Love-Based Feminine Marketing

THE ART OF GROWING A 6-FIGURE
BUSINESS WITHOUT HUSTLE,
GRIND, OR FORCE

by Julie Foucht

Love-Based Feminine Marketing:

Love-Based Feminine Marketing:
The Art of Growing a 6-Figure Business Without
Hustle, Grind, or Force.

Copyright © 2020 by Julie Foucht. All rights reserved. Printed in the United States of America. No part of this book may be reproduced or transmitted in any manner or by any means, electronically or mechanically, including photocopying, recording, retrieval system, without prior written permission from the author, except in the case of brief quotations embodied in a review. For information, address Julie Foucht, PO BOX 10430, Prescott AZ 86304.

This book may be purchased for educational, business, or sales promotional use. For information, please email info@lovebasedpublishing.com.

ISBN 978-1-945363-17-7

Library of Congress Control Number: 2020940587

Contents

Love-Based Feminine Marketing I

The Art of Growing a 6-Figure Business Without Hustle, Grind, or Force I

DEDICATION 1

NOTE FROM THE PUBLISHER 3

INTRODUCTION—WHY THIS BOOK? 7

CHAPTER 1 13
  Being Raised a Girl

CHAPTER 2 19
  Who Am I Going to Be?

CHAPTER 3 23
  The Keeper of My Wisdom

CHAPTER 4 27
  The First Reading

CHAPTER 5 31
  Leave or die

CHAPTER 6 37
  Breathing Without Fear

CHAPTER 7 41
  Connecting with Our Highest Self

CHAPTER 8..51
Connecting with the Energy of Your Business

CHAPTER 9..61
"The Wound Is the Place the Light Enters Us."

CHAPTER 10..67
The Wound Recovery Process

CHAPTER 11..77
Connecting with Your Tribe

CHAPTER 12..83
The Inner Saboteurs: Resistance, Perfectionism, Indecision, Overwhelm, and Procrastination

CHAPTER 13..91
Caring for the Vessel

CHAPTER 14..97
Creating Your Inner Mastermind

CHAPTER 15...103
The Dance of The Feminine and The Masculine

CHAPTER 16...109
Marketing Strategy 1: Warm Market Reach-Out … The Feminine Way

CHAPTER 17...119
Marketing Strategy 2: Face to Face

CHAPTER 18...133
Marketing Strategy 3: Content Marketing

CHAPTER 19...147
Marketing Strategy 4: Establishing Expertise from the Stage

CHAPTER 20 .... Love-Based Feminine Marketing: 161
Making Friends with Money

CHAPTER 21 168
How Good Can You Stand It?

RESOURCES 173

OTHER BOOKS IN THE LOVE-BASED BUSINESS SERIES 175

ABOUT THE AUTHOR 183
ABOUT Julie Foucht

Dedication

Thanks to the principles outlined in this book, my life today is rich and abundant. As I reflect back on my journey, there are so many people to thank.

To my amazing clients—the women who rise every day and recommit themselves to their Soul-work, allowing their Divine Feminine selves to lead, so they can bring their magic into the world. I am in awe of you each and every day. It is my honor to walk the path with you.

To my teachers—the men and women whose shoulders I stand on. Loretta, Cecilia, Maria, Susan, Kendra, Connor, and Jeffery, thank you for sharing your wisdom and seeing the best in me, encouraging me to grow into the woman I am today.

To the ones who wounded me—it was not a happy or comfortable experience; yet, without you, I would not have developed my strength. My power would have remained hidden. I won't name names, but on a soul level, I am grateful.

To my wonderful friends who walked the path with me and continue to light my way—Marla, Lisa, Cyndi, Laurie, Janelle, Lizzie, and Ramona. Thank you for being there for me, encouraging me, and loving me in my imperfection.

To my soul-sisters—Therese and Lindsay, who hold me to my path every day, inspire me to expand beyond my comfort zone, and push my edges continuously. I love you ladies.

To my husband—thank you for holding me. You are my rock. I have the courage to do this work, to go out in the world and proclaim my magic, to give my all to the work, because I have you to come home to. I love you to the moon and back.

To my children and stepchildren—you taught me to love unconditionally. You bring richness and joy to my life. I marvel at the individuals you have each become.

To my littles—my grandchildren. You are the lights of my life. I'm so delighted that you chose our family to join. I'm so looking forward to who you will be and enjoying (almost) every minute of the journey.

If I've forgotten someone in this dedication, I am sorry. You are remembered and honored by my soul.

Note From The Publisher

This book is part of an entrepreneurial mission to inspire as many people as possible to shift form living a fear-based life to living a love-based life: that is, living and making decisions from a place of love-based emotions like abundance, hope, gratitude, peace, and trust rather than from a place of fear-based emotions like scarcity, fear, shame, guilt, and anger.

Michele PW, author of the first Love-Based Business Books (*Love-Based Copywriting Method: The Philosophy Behind Writing Copy that Attracts, Inspires and Invites; Love-Based Copywriting System: A Step-by-Step Process to Master Writing Copy That Attracts, Inspires and Invites; Love-Based Online Marketing: Campaigns to Grow a Business You Love & that Loves You Back; Love-Based Money & Mindset: Make the Money You Desire Without Selling Your Soul; Love-Based Goals: Your Guide to Living Your Purpose & Passion*) and founder of the Love-Based Copywriting Company, established the Love-Based Copy Philosophy when she first saw the title of a book her friend Susan Liddy wrote, "Love-Based Marketing." (Michele immediately thought of "Love-Based Copy," and then asked herself what the opposite of Love-Based Copy would be, which is fear-based ... and then, the entire philosophy downloaded into her.) She now considers herself its steward as it grows, flowing from business topics into other areas of life, including health, relationships, creativity, and career.

As the deliverers of the Love-Based Philosophy message, we believe it's our role to educate people on living a love-based life—and, in the case of this book, building a love-based business.

A lot of what we consider "traditional business" is built on a foundation of fear. But you don't have to build your business that way—in fact, this book is all about building a business that aligns with who you are, at your very core—and doing so from a place of love.

Now, just to be clear, being love-based doesn't mean you don't feel fear-based emotions. On the contrary, people who have embraced love-based businesses and lives in fact DO fully feel all emotions, whether love-based or fear-based. There IS definitely a place for fear-based emotions in our human existence (believe it or not, those feelings exist to help you), so rather than fight them, the idea is to really feel them, and let them move through you.

Being love-based simply means you embody love-based emotions, in your life and in your business.

As this particular book focuses on business, and the following tenets of living a love-based life are important to understand:

- 💜 Love and honor yourself, and create your life and your business around loving and honoring yourself.

- 💜 Love what you do in the world.

- 💜 Receive the money, abundance, prosperity, and gifts that are your birthright.

- Realize that just because you love what you do in the world doesn't mean that you love every aspect of everything you do each day. Part of living a love-based life (and building a love-based business) means being open to the complete experience of living. Sometimes it means making hard choices.

You have a choice about the way you build your business.

By investing in this book, you've made the choice to learn about whether you can join us on the love-based path, and shift into a love-based way of living (and working) … one that perfectly matches who you are, when you're at your very best.

Welcome, and happy reading! We look forward to walking alongside you.

Love-Based Feminine Marketing:

Introduction—Why This Book?

Historically, a woman's value was measured by her ability to attract a husband and produce heirs. Women were taught to be "nice" and submissive, so they could "make a good match" and "be taken care of."

That was the generational legacy my dad carried on when he "raised his girls to be taken care of."

But throughout this same history, women have challenged that perception of a woman's role.

Midwives and healers were once held in high regard, until the witch hunts began. Then, they were accused of sorcery and ultimately drowned or burned at the stake.

The pioneers of the Women's Rights Movement of the late 19th century were heavily criticized as "semi-feminine." They were accused of "disrupting the natural order" of things, and it was widely believed that there was something wrong with them physically that caused them to do so.

When the Feminist Movement of the 1960s hit, more and more women entered the workforce. But opportunities for advancing to the highest ranks remained very few. (Even today, women *still* make less than men working similar jobs.)

Because women in the modern workforce had few female role models, they began to emulate men in business. To achieve status and promotions, they became men in pencil skirts.

And then, as women began starting their own businesses, they continued to imitate the way men do business: find a problem, determine a solution, outline the required number of sales to create the desired profit, create action steps, and drive, drive, drive until profit is realized.

Women crammed themselves into a box, wearing suits with big shoulders and talking "like the boys" (or taking a back seat to the boys).

But what happens when a woman dares to step out of that mode?

When she decides to activate her feminine energy and bring all of who she is to her work?

That's what this book is about—choosing a NEW way of doing business—a way that is directed from within, birthed from your connection to your Divine Feminine, and supported by the actions of your Divine Masculine.

By the time you're finished reading, you'll have discovered how to connect directly to your Highest Self—the inner manifestation of your Divine Feminine. You'll also know how to empower your Divine Masculine to take the action needed to bring your vision for your business into reality in the physical plane.

By igniting a sacred dance between your Divine Feminine and your Divine Masculine, your business, programs, and marketing all become a reflection of Source/God/The Universe that exists within you.

And in learning to connect with your Highest Self, you open a door to receiving assistance from all kinds of unseen "helpers" (I speak from experience, here).

We come into this world with the understanding that we are connected to all things and beings. Look into the eyes of a newborn, and you can see their connection to Source/God. You can see their understanding.

Then, we begin to forget.

We are taught to think with our brain—to problem solve with our head and ignore the messages from our body. We forget our connection to the spirit world. We forget that we are of Source, and Source resides in us.

This is part of the differentiation that humans go through. We endure a series of experiences that create wounds, and though them, we develop skills and talents that prepare us perfectly for the work we are meant to do on the planet.

Therefore, once our education is complete, we must learn to connect again.

First to Source, through your Highest Self ... thereby opening the door to the spirit world.

Then, to the Energy of Your Business, which has its own signature and vibration.

Next, to the Energy of Your Tribe—the people you are here to serve. Doing so enables you to be absolutely clear about what you bring to their lives and how they need you to speak, thereby leaving a trail of spiritual breadcrumbs they can follow to find you, as you draw their souls to you.

Then, to the Energetic Representative of your body ... your Body Singer. She will guide you in ensuring that your vessel is fully tuned, so you can do your best work.

Next, with your Inner Mastermind Counsel, for guidance.

And finally, to the Energy of Money, to create an abundant, juicy, wildly successful life.

Connecting allows you to create. To give birth.

And that is the work of the Feminine.

It is the only path to true innovation and thought leadership.

It is the path to abundance.

To help you take the teachings even deeper, I've included several exercises and resources throughout this book. As you read, you can access all of them and more (meditations, checklists, and other tools to support you) via my Resource Center, here: JULIEFOUCHT.COM/FMRESOURCES.

Let's get started!

Love-Based Feminine Marketing:

# Chapter 1
BEING RAISED A GIRL

Summer in Washington state is a precious thing. After so many winter days under a blanket of clouds and darkness that rolls in around 4:00 pm, the light of summer is transformative.

While organizing a family gathering one day, I remember feeling the sun caress my bare arms … how it sparkled on the blades of grass, inviting me to sink down onto the warm, earthy cover … to let go and just *be*, for a moment.

Yet, even during that moment of peace, a part of me stayed on guard, watching intently for danger. The words I allowed to come out of my mouth were measured. I couldn't feel my heart, under the layers of protection I had built around it.

Even as an adult, I could still feel the weight of being the oldest, and therefore, responsible for everyone else.

As the "outsider" in a family of five children, I could also still feel the loneliness. I was different than my two brothers: the "golden child" and the dependable one. I was different than my two sisters: the troubled one and the "baby."

I was used to being "not quite": not quite good enough … not quite lovable enough … not quite capable enough … not quite worthy enough.

Still, there I was in charge again, desperately trying to make everyone happy.

I sat with my dad at the picnic table outside of the roadside café I'd chosen for lunch. We were enjoying a bit of small talk about the kids and the day as I absentmindedly ran my fingers across the bubbles in the rough finish of the table.

"You know," my dad said suddenly, in reflection. "I raised my boys to get along in the world. I raised my girls to be taken care of."

I let the words sink in.

My dad, who as a boy rode a horse through Los Angeles (when it was all orange groves) to get to the beach for the day. Who forged his mother's signature to join the Navy at 17 and fought in the Korean War. Who returned from war and slept under a bridge in Seattle for six months before going home to California. Who worked as a long-haul truck driver from the time I was five through 16, gone three weeks out of every month.

My dad, who never in his life followed traditional rules, had stuck to the script that had been handed down for generations in our family (and in many others).

Until the mid-1850s, married women in the United States were not allowed to own property, open a bank account, or hire a lawyer. Un-married women had limited options for employment, and if they did marry, they were expected to stop working. Their husbands then took ownership of their property.

The best chance for a good life came from being nice, attractive, and "marriageable"—to be "people-pleasers," so a good man would choose them.

To this day, women carry these unspoken rules in our DNA, passed from generation to generation without a whisper.

And that means, as we women strive to make our way in the world, the wounds of our ancestors haunt us. Without even knowing it, we replay the patterns that have been woven into our very cell structure, struggling to understand why it seems so hard to break the people-pleaser tendencies that keep us from being fully authentic, powerful, and successful.

Growing up, our family lived in a resort mountain town of 300 full-time residents. During winter, it frequently snowed heavily.

My brothers were always encouraged to work. When it snowed, they were sent out with shovels to clear the roofs of neighboring cabins to prevent collapse. The owners, who lived down in the "flatlands," happily paid them for this service.

When I was a little older, my parents opened the first-and-only gas station/garage in town to supplement my dad's income as a truck driver. My mother and brothers (ages 10 and 11) ran the station while my dad, still working as a truck driver, went on cross-country delivery trips.

I was envious of my brothers' strength, bravery, and know-how. My mind searched for ways a girl, small and helpless like me, could make money, too. When I suggested I could help alongside my brothers, I was told it was "too dangerous." There were too many hazardous tools and, definitely too much dirt and grease.

Secretly, I was grateful to be able to stay inside with a warm fire with a book to escape into. Nonetheless, I was ever intrigued by the thought of being *able* to make money for myself.

I had plans for my life, too.

I would go to college.

I would become a wealthy actress.

I would be interviewed by Merv Griffin.

I would take over his show and change the world of television forever!

I knew I could do it. After all, my mother said I could do *anything* I wanted. (Well, besides being a singer. Or dancer. But *anything* else, she was sure!)

My dad? Like he said ... he only thought of preparing me to be "taken care of."

And the words he spoke that day at our family gathering were the closest he would ever come to an apology.

Love-Based Feminine Marketing:

Chapter 2
WHO AM I GOING TO BE?

Five months after my high school graduation, I married my high school boyfriend, Scott.

I remember him confessing how happy he was to be married, because it meant he didn't have to chase me anymore. Of course, that didn't mean he was done chasing other women. But now, he could come home to me and I could "take care of him."

The marriage produced four children in quick succession. We were both so young and overwhelmed.

When our youngest was in preschool, Scott started his own construction firm and begged me to be the bookkeeper ("just until it took off"). Since I stayed home with the kids, he was able to control me with money.

It was not my dream. I actually hated the work and the isolation.

But he loved it! It kept me tied to him and away from other people. It gave him even more authority over me. He told me, "We are equal partners, but if we don't agree on something, I get the final say."

In other words, we were equal partners *when I agreed with him*.

Truthfully, Scott was a narcissist and a bully.

His first affair (or the first I was aware of) tore me up inside. I felt like a doll made of paper-thin china: any move I made might just crack me wide open and I would be so broken that I would never be put back together again.

He told me it was actually a "good thing." It helped him see what was important in life. He also said if I had been paying more attention to him, serving his needs, having more sex, and filling the empty hole in him, he wouldn't have needed the affair.

It was, then, my fault.

I was defective. We could have a good marriage, he said, if I would just "fix myself."

And then he said the issue was over and forbade me to talk about it.

I knew what I needed to do.

Leave.

But I couldn't. I felt helpless. Alone.

I stayed in the marriage because I didn't see another way. I had a high school education and four children. I was sure that, if I left, he and his mother would take my children away from me. There was no way I could earn enough money on my own to pay for daycare and put food in their mouths.

I stayed because I was afraid—afraid of the world, and of not being able to take care of myself.

I stayed because there is no cure for being born a girl.

I stayed, ignoring the verbal abuse. I built walls to protect myself from the emotional abuse. I made excuses for the physical abuse. *It only happens a couple of times a year. I've never had to go to the hospital. I've never had visible bruises. It's not that bad.*

I felt weak and ashamed. So, I ignored the chaos and fashioned a mask I could wear in public.

And I wore that mask well.

I was the chair of our school bond and levy campaigns, winning a multi-million-dollar bond to build a new high school (one that had lost in five previous elections).

I chaired a local community building festival that drew 5000 people in a town of 20,000.

I became friends with the superintendent of schools and the police chief.

I became a mini-celebrity in our community. (Really, people would meet me and say, "Oh, you're *her!*")

It felt good to be respected—acknowledged for what I *could* do.

But then, I would tiptoe home, hoping nothing would set Scott off, causing him to explode.

One day, I was preparing for a dinner party with friends when a question hit me like a punch in the gut:

"Who am I going to be when they get here?"

If our guests saw the weak, watchful woman I was at home, they would lose all respect. If I was the magnetic, get-things-done powerhouse I was in the community, Scott would fume. Someone (me) would end up hurt.

That's when I knew I couldn't hide anymore. Something had to change.

Chapter 3
THE KEEPER OF MY WISDOM

That's when I met Loretta.

Introduced by a friend, she was a gifted psychic and Reiki master. I didn't really have any idea what to expect when I first went to meet her. I was full of hope and trepidation, and desperate for answers.

How could I continue to live the way I was living? How could I have a life in a house with a man who was only happy when I was not? Who broke my things, punched walls, threw me up the stairs, and raised his fist in my face to evoke cooperation?

I entered her apartment a wounded bird—a waif who hardly even knew her own name anymore.

I immediately noticed a tapestry hanging in the entry way of Sheva, the Goddess. She had several arms and three heads. She was woven into the deep-blue fabric with gold and red thread. It *felt* like magic … like she could look straight into one's soul.

An enormous grand piano archly filled most of the space in the living room. Books spilled from the open drawers of a TV cabinet onto tables, floors, and one corner of the couch. Dozens of ceramic angels hovered protectively around the room. The only surface not covered with angels or books was the piano.

More questions: What would Loretta say to me? Would she be able to look into my soul and see all the darkness? Would she tell me that all the horrible things my husband said were true? Would she see that I am a horrible mother? Know that my daughter hated me, calling me a cow? Know that my son hated me, too, and pushed me like his dad? Would she scold me for wasting her time?

My shoulders furled forward as I tried to make myself as small as possible. I set my face in a mask of neutrality and slipped into the hidden places of my soul, leaving only a peephole to the outer world that would allow me access to Loretta.

And then she entered the room, everything about her sensual, sexual, warm. Older than me by ten years, her face was still nearly unlined and sported just the right amount of makeup. Her brown hair curled at her shoulders and her eyes were wide and expressive. Her skirt floated around her body and her loose top revealed just a hint of cleavage.

We introduced ourselves, settling onto the couch. "Tell me about your beliefs," Lorretta asked, speaking each careful word clearly. Her voice was soft and welcoming.

"I believe in God," I said, holding my hands together tightly. *Don't cross your arms*, I think. *It looks closed, unfriendly.* "I was raised Catholic. I left the church just before my youngest was born. I meditate. I talk to God, but not as often as I would like. I do my own dream analysis to try to figure out what they are telling me." It all just tumbled out.

I saw Loretta shift her gaze toward the piano. I instinctually wanted to turn to see what she was looking at, but I was afraid. I was guarded—she could be an enemy or an ally. I kept my eyes on her face, looking for signs of anger.

"I'm sorry," she said, "but there is a great big angel behind you."

Umm ... yes, I thought. *There are ceramic angels everywhere.*

I glanced behind me anyway, seeing only the piano. No angels.

"He is about eight feet tall and is carrying a sword," Loretta tells me.

It was suddenly very warm in her apartment. The back of my neck tingled the way it does when someone is watching me. Suddenly, I was Alice, and I'd stepped through the looking glass into a world that looked like mine, yet wasn't.

I am going crazy, I thought. *I don't want to be in this house with this woman discussing the possibility of leaving my husband. Someone has set a spell on me or woken me from a dream into a horrible reality. I may split in two and die if someone doesn't help me.*

"This angel is a spirit guide for you," Loretta continues. "He is here to guard you from danger and remind you to speak the truth. He says you and I must always speak the truth to one another, no matter how uncomfortable it is."

An angel is right behind me, I think. *He has a big sword and is guarding me.* I closed my eyes and could feel his breath in my hair, his cold sword at my back. The air rushed from my lungs.

For the first time in as long as I could remember, I realized I wasn't alone and I didn't have to be so on guard.

Loretta was watching me—my hope and perhaps, my executioner.

I did not know if she would teach me how to live or, condemn me to die.

Loretta smiled. "I can work with you," she said. "Come see me on Thursday."

And I was dismissed.

Chapter 4
THE FIRST READING

That Thursday, Loretta and I sat together on an intricately woven silk mat on the floor of her tiny apartment.

Pulling out a deck of cards from a velvet pouch, Loretta said, "I keep them covered, so they don't pick up stray energy."

I had never seen a tarot deck before. The one in front of me exuded the same warmth and "earthiness" I felt around Loretta. The edges were worn with use and the back side was covered in intricate crosses and stylized fruit. I shuffled the deck and Loretta began spreading the cards across the cloth. I instinctively held my hand a few inches over the cards, noticing how the temperature varied between them.

"Ask your question," she murmured. "Spirit will answer through the cards."

This is real, I thought. My stomach clenched and I fought back tears. A question rose like vomit in my throat. I desperately pushed it down, to keep it inside. I *can't ask that,* I thought. *I won't.*

"Breathe," commanded Loretta, "and ask if you should leave your husband."

I won't.

"Can I ask if I can stay, and stay alive?"

"You can ask whatever you like."

I formed the words of the safest question I could think of: "How do I stay?"

"Now choose a card," she said. "But don't turn it over."

I passed my left hand over the deck until I could feel my palm tingling. I pulled the card and handed it to Loretta. Repeat. The second card was warm. The third was so hot, I thought it might burn my palm. I continued choosing cards until Loretta stopped me. She started placing them in front of me, following a specific pattern. She turned over the first card—the High Priestess.

"This is you," she said.

The picture was of a young woman with columns on either side of her. She looked straight ahead, unblinking. The column on the left was black, and the one on the right, white.

"This is Persephone," Loretta continued, "the queen of the underworld. Persephone was kidnapped by the king of the underworld, who carried her deep into his world. Her mother had warned her not to eat anything there, but Persephone was so hungry, she neglected the advice and was ultimately tricked into eating six pomegranate seeds. See, here on the card, the pomegranate?"

The air was filled with the magic of the story carried by Loretta's voice. She shifted and the soft folds of her skirt rustled. There seemed to be a bubble around us, sitting on the floor with the cards resting on the patterned silk between us. The High Priestess was in the center. Other cards were lying above and below. Four to the right side in a row, four surrounding Persephone, and two crossing over above her.

"The Celtic Cross," Loretta informed me, pointing to one of the cards. The air tingled with the feeling of the dream world—that special place between wakefulness and sleep where anything can happen. Yet I was fully awake and completely aware of what was happening in that bubble.

The world outside our small circle faded to a whisper of birds singing. They provided a soft melody accompanying the sound of Loretta's voice. I was drawn, like a fairy to the soft sighs of a sleeping newborn infant, into the story.

"Persephone escapes and returns to the upper world, and with her comes the sun and new growth—the return of spring to the land. Now, as punishment for eating the six pomegranate seeds, she must return to the underworld each fall and rule the people for six months. The land above becomes dark and falls dormant, waiting for her return."

Loretta pressed the card into my hand. "Persephone learned to live in both worlds—the physical and the spirit—one foot in each. This is what *you* must do. Both are equally important. Neither is more important than the other. You must learn to do this."

She turned the next card over—the nine of swords. "This is your present situation."

"This is the card of tears and nightmares. The swords are piercing their target with inescapable pain. You are just waking to the nightmare of this life. Just becoming aware."

"This is the immediate challenge." She turned the two of swords. "You have a choice to make, but don't yet realize it. See how the woman is blindfolded? If you choose to take the blindfold off, you will have to decide …"

The cards unfolded the story. Loretta, a supportive figure. Friends as advisors and companions on my journey. A decision to be made.

For now, I could stay, just as things were.

But I had a much more dangerous question looming over me. The one I didn't want to ask … didn't want to take the blindfold off to see …

How do I LIVE?

Chapter 5
LEAVE OR DIE

Ten sessions.

That was the number Lorretta and I had agreed on to work together, and I had done everything she asked during each and every one.

Meeting for our eleventh session, we both acknowledged (without saying a word) that our journey had come to an end.

I felt wrapped in 1000 narrow threads, each one cutting just a tiny bit into my skin. Together, they kept me bound and safe—safe from my own longing to be free. Safe from falling off the bridge of the unknown. Safe from ruining …

What? My façade of a life?

I was lying on her bed, which faced east, on top of the multi-colored tapestry she used as a spread.

"They told me you need to have your head in the west, your feet east," she sighed. "I've never had to change the direction of my bed for a client before."

I said nothing.

I'd spent twenty years unsuccessfully honing my ability to say just the right thing … to spin the words into a shield that dispels anger and brings peace. I'd rarely been successful. When I tried with Scott, his anger intensified. The raised fists, broken furniture, and holes in the walls all gave testament to my inability to find the right words.

And so, when Lorretta sighed, I stayed quiet.

Lorretta sat on the floor, her skirt pooling around her bare feet. *She is beautiful,* I think.

"Now close your eyes," she instructed me. "Let the music carry you."

I entered a waking dream. As images appeared, I told Lorretta what I saw.

A long line of men, foot soldiers in some ancient war. They are weaving through a deep forest. The light is grey, filtered by the trees. The leaves of the trees are moist, heavy with afternoon fog.

In the middle of the line is a woman. She is wearing a tattered grey skirt with a thick brown cloak. Her hands are bound behind her. Her face is streaked with soot and tears.

The men's faces are stern, and a little afraid. The man behind the woman clutches the rope that binds her. His eyes never leave her back as he urges her forward.

The image changed. And changed again.

Finally, I was in a garden, and I felt safe.

It is summer. The air is thick with sunshine, warm and inviting. I hear a bird somewhere in the distance.

There is a stone bench in the garden, next to a small pond.

I sit.

My Highest Self joins me.

I sense her energy before seeing an image. A pulsing in my womb, in my face. My fingertips tingle.

A white light presses in on me and a face appears. Serene, strong, compassionate. She wears a golden crown and curls of the same color frame her face.

"Welcome, dear one," she says.

I am now on the ground at her feet. She is sitting on a throne, patient, waiting for me to ask the question.

Finally, I am ready. All the pain, the desire, the longing pour out of me as I ask, "Must I leave my marriage?"

My Highest Self smiles. She pulls a roll of paper forward and unrolls it. It is a series of maps printed on translucent paper, so that when one is placed on top of another, it adds to the picture below. When they are all laid out, one on top of the other, they tell such a complex story, it's nearly impossible to comprehend.

But when separated, the message is clear. As each page is added to the next, the story grows.

"You do not have to leave," she says. "You can stay and die."

I look toward the maps and see the red bloodstains that seep from one to the next.

"Your death," she continues, "will seep into the lives of those who come after. It will continue to stain the next generation and the next."

"What is my alternative?" I ask.

"Leave. Take my hand and follow me into the unknown future. Come alive, my darling."

She directs my attention back to the maps. As she lifts them, the red disappears.

"These are the past," she tells me. "All the pain and fear are done. Let us look forward."

She traces a circle with one long, thin finger on the map, pointing to a new home. "Let go of the old one," she says. "It is filled with ghosts of the past."

"You have now been brave enough to ask the question. This is the hardest part. There will be days when you think it's harder. You will feel broken and lost. But the question ... that is truly the hardest."

Yes, I think. I have never been brave enough to truly ask. And now, I have an answer.

"Will I ever find someone to love me?" I ask, surprising myself.

She giggles. "Yes," she says. "First, it will be you who loves you. And then, you will find him."

Love-Based Feminine Marketing:

Chapter 6
BREATHING WITHOUT FEAR

And so, I left.

At first, I trusted no one, nothing.

All men are lying to their wives. All wives are living in a pretend world. There are no rules. I don't know how to act. I don't know how to live.

I imagined myself a pile of wet leaves—cold and brittle on top, rotting underneath.

I rented a home and hid away.

I'd taken very little with me: one piece of furniture (my old, green sofa) and some pictures of the kids to hang on the walls. A friend had given me some old director's chairs that I paired with a folding table in the dining room; that was pretty much all I had.

One day, I walked in the door and noticed the tabletop was stained yellow.

I should cover that with a tablecloth, I thought. *But I have no money to purchase one.*

The house *felt* so different.

My whole marriage taught me to hide my emotions. I had learned the true meaning of fear and sadness.

I had learned to be on guard. To feign happiness around the things my husband loved. I had let my tears fall endlessly into the soil, watering my garden when no one was watching.

I had learned to sob, silently, without moving. Because even that would make him fly into a rage.

"Why can't you just be happy that I have something I want," he would say. "Why can't you just be happy supporting my business, my dreams?"

In the meantime, I had buried my own dream.

I had also learned to watch closely for signs of his mood shifting, a clear indication that fists or books or dishes were about to fly.

All of this flashed through my mind as I walked through the door of my new home.

I didn't know what I was feeling. It was so new.

Then I realized … *it was a lack of fear.*

I exhaled.

I am safe.

I had my answer to my first question: should I leave?

And I had done it.

Now, it was time to tackle the next big question:

How do I come back to life?

Love-Based Feminine Marketing:

Chapter 7
CONNECTING WITH OUR HIGHEST SELF

In every story, there is a moment when the heroine can no longer "refuse the call."

I had come to that moment the day I took a breath without fear.

Because I was *free*.

When the fear finally left me, I could begin my quest of discovery: *What am I here for? Why was I born into these times?*

My journey, like all our journeys, had challenges to overcome, miles to travel, and lots of companions along the way.

My guide, through it all, has been my Highest Self.

You see, your Highest Self is the part of you that *never* forgets how we are all connected to Source, even as we are taught to forget, to individualize, and to live in the physical world.

She is the one who walks the spirit world and speaks with angels. She is the one who is able to see wisdom in wounds and the light of your highest and best future.

She clearly sees all the threads that make up the tapestry of your life—the ones that reach back to the previous lives your soul has lived to bring forth memories into this one. The ones that pull from your ancestors, tangling their beliefs and limitations with yours. The ones that wind forward into a legacy for those who will come after you—your children and grandchildren.

She carries the maps that mark your journey through life and notes the changes when you make decisions.

She has, on her belt, the key to the vault where your life contracts with others are stored. The contracts of wounding, of support, and of love.

She tends to the sacred garden within you—a place where you can meet your unseen guides and guardians. A place where the wounded and hidden parts of you can be called forth out of the shadows for reintegration. A place where magic spells and healing rooms and spiritual connections exist!

She is the gatekeeper to your soul's knowing, and she speaks your soul's guidance.

Yet, in modern society, we are taught to ignore this keeper of wisdom. To think with our heads, to create lists of pros and cons, and to decide *logically* based on information gathered in the physical world.

Trusting a spiritual version of yourself, one who has all the answers, seems a little like "magical thinking," right?

After all, we live in a world where driving ourselves to exhaustion is a badge of honor. Being overwhelmed and having too much to do has become a standard by which we judge ourselves. We have huge TO-DO lists and are constantly in ACTION.

The Feminine Way is different.

It requires leaning inward. Finding the connection to your Highest Self *first*. Postponing action, until it's the correct time. Trusting Source.

How? I'm sharing one of my favorite methods with you below. But before we get into that, I want to address a question I hear all the time:

How do you know if you're actually speaking to your Highest Self, or if it's just all in your head?

The more time you spend with your Higher Self, the easier it will become to recognize her voice and feel her energy. Then, you'll know when she is guiding you.

My Higher Self is light. She is always, even when angry, the greatest advocate of my highest good. She is non-judgmental, offering vision and wisdom, never condemnation. She is me, as pure love.

She tells me now to tell you that she is "a vision of light, glistening in the dew drops of a thousand fairy tears."

Of course, *your* Highest Self may appear differently.

And know that sometimes, you will ask your Highest Self for guidance, but will get no answer. That used to drive me crazy! I'd ask, "What am I supposed to be doing with my life?"

And my Highest Self would say, "It's not time for you to know yet."

Now, looking back, I realize I hadn't been on the journey long enough to receive an answer to that question. I hadn't developed the skills I needed to do the work. If I had received the answer then, I would have attempted to create the Art of Feminine Marketing (more about this later) before its time. And, I would have failed.

I also know that, as I continue to grow and evolve, so will my work. I don't know exactly what it will evolve into, but I have learned to trust that *the knowledge will be given to me when the timing is correct.*

I know that my connection to Source, through my Highest Self, will provide me the answers I need when I need them.

And, that's why I want to help YOU connect with yours.

Generally speaking, you can do so through a combination of guided meditation and journaling.

Every time I write, I feel my Highest Self sitting with me. She sometimes asks if she can help and I gratefully accept.

Even right now, this many pages into this book, my ego is full of doubt and criticism.

But my Highest Self is calm, graceful, and light.

I'm not sure what comes next. But she is.

"It is time," she says, "for the reader to meet her Highest Self."

Exercise: Connect with Your Highest Self

***DOWNLOAD AN AUDIO VERSION OF THIS GUIDED MEDITATION HERE: <u>JULIEFOUCHT.COM/FMRESOURCES/</u>. ***

Sit or lay comfortably in a place where you will not be disturbed for 20 minutes or more. Turn off any computer programs that might distract you with alerts. Switch your cell phone to silent. Turn off anything that might distract you from meeting with your Highest Self. Have a journal and pen or word document open to record the details of your meeting after the meditation.

If you are adept at meditation and journaling, you may keep your fingers on your keyboard and transcribe your journey and conversation with your Highest Self as it occurs.

Let's get started.

Close your eyes and take a deep breath in. Slowly let it out, bringing your attention inward. Breathe in again, feeling the air fill your body with life-sustaining oxygen. Blow the air all the way out of your body through your mouth. Let outside noise fade away, allowing you to more deeply enter the inner realm. Breathe in again, welcoming love and healing into your body, and blowing out all the stress and negativity that clings to you.

As you continue to breathe in and out, imagine you are standing on a beach. Notice what the waves look like, what color the water is. Notice the feel of the air on your skin and the sounds of the beach around you.

Now, notice a door, standing all by itself, on the beach. Nothing behind it, nothing in front. Just a door.

What color is it? What is it made of? Notice the doorknob. What is its color and shape?

In a moment, you are going to go through the door into your own secret, private garden. This is a sacred space where only you and those entities who are there for your highest good can enter.

Open the door and step into your garden.

Take a few moments to explore. Notice the types of plants, the sun or moonlight. Are there any animals or magical beings in your garden? What are you feeling as you explore?

Now, notice the path in front of you. Follow it as it guides you deeper and deeper into the very center of the garden—the most sacred place where you are most strongly connected to Source.

As you enter the center of your garden, take a moment to look around. Now, you see a place to sit comfortably and have a conversation. Sit and ask, "May I speak with my Highest Self?"

She may come to you fully formed, in lots of detail, or wrapped in veils of mist, so you can barely make out her shape. She may be energy or an impression in the air. However your Highest Self comes to you is perfect for this moment.

Greet your Highest Self, invite her to sit and have a conversation with you.

Ask her any questions you want—here are some ideas:

- Highest Self, what is your promise to me?

- Highest Self, what do I need to pay attention to that I'm not?

- Highest Self, what are my greatest strengths?

- Highest Self, where do I need to seek support?

- Highest Self, who do I need to enroll in my vision?

- 💜 Highest Self, what do I need to know about myself, that I don't already know?

- 💜 Highest Self, how can I be of greater service today?

- 💜 Highest Self, what do I need to know about my business right now?

- 💜 Highest Self, what is my next right step in creating a business that fully supports all of who I am?

Again, these are just suggestions. Ask any question that comes up for you during the course of the conversation.

And of course, listen for your Highest Self's answers. Generally, the answers are in the form of the immediate thoughts you have after asking your question. Don't question or second guess what you receive.

When you feel complete, thank your Highest Self for her time, bringing your conversation to a natural close.

Hug your Highest Self, knowing that she is part of you, always available, and always supporting you.

Step back onto the path and follow it back through your garden to your door. Know that you can come back to this place any time you want.

As you step through the door, feel yourself come fully back into your body. Notice the way your body feels as you breathe in and out. Slowly move your body, feeling the air on your skin and the ground beneath you.

Now, pick up your journal and record your journey in detail. Write down everything you can remember.

Like any relationship, your connection to your Highest Self will strengthen as you give it time and attention. Carve time into your calendar to check in with your Highest Self several times a week. Get to know her.

Love-Based Feminine Marketing:

Chapter 8
CONNECTING WITH THE ENERGY OF YOUR BUSINESS

After letting go of fear, the whole world opened up for me. I felt free to dream, to create, and to be all of who I am!

One day, I sat on the floor with my journal in front of me. The sun streamed in creating beams of light. They reminded me of the lazy days of summer as a child, when the sunlight sparkled through the leaves of the oak tree outside my bedroom window.

I felt a surge of nostalgia rise up from my belly into my heart, not for what was, but for what could be.

I began to write.

I created a vision for my life five years in the future. It included a house on the beach, a cat and a dog, happy kids, a loving partner, and a business all my own. I didn't know what that business would look like yet, but I knew what I wanted to do.

I wanted to empower other women.

I was beginning to learn that I could take care of myself. That I could earn money in the world. That I didn't need someone to take care of me. That I was capable.

I knew there were other women who felt stuck, too. Just like I had, in situations that were not life *giving*. I wanted to give them the strength to do what I had done, without waiting 20 years to do it.

I carried this vision with me when I moved back to sunny California, got a job where I was appreciated and started to date, quickly moving on from anyone who disrespected me.

Then, I discovered the world of Life Coaching and I knew I had found my place. All those years of asking, "What should I be doing with my life?" came into focus. This was it—*this* was how I was going to empower other women!

But I still had miles to go and tons to learn before the true nature of the work revealed itself. So, I embarked on the coaching journey, earning my coaching certification from The Coaches Training Institute, the school that sets the standard for the International Coaching Federation.

And for ten years, I coached women entrepreneurs, teaching them the masculine side of business building (the actions necessary for success). As I taught strategy, I'd slip in my magic, my "woo-woo," quietly (and without ever admitting it in my marketing).

Then, I heard a quote that changed my life.

"Create your business as a reflection of the Divine; then, talking to your biz is talking to the Divine." - Cory Michelle

My heart shivered when I heard the words.

Up until that point, I'd been secretive about the other half of my success … the feminine beingness. I didn't talk with my clients about connecting with Source or allowing Spirit to guide.

Cory's words stirred something in me.

I quickly jotted them down in my notebook before slipping into the swirl of emotions that flashed through my body.

My hands tingled, a sign that I was picking up an energetic message. My heart cracked open, as if a bolt of lightning had pierced my protective armor.

I felt curious. Excited.

One thought resonated through my body:

What would happen if I could talk to my business?

A shiver of goosebumps—no, *truth*bumps—ran down my arms and across my shoulders.

I felt the tingle of another.

Not a person, or a spirit. An energy seeking me.

My legs began to melt into the chair, my body relaxing, welcoming.

The Other tentatively brushed against my energy.

"Will you be the one?" It whispered. *"Will you bring me into this physical realm?"*

Before this moment, my business was based on nuts-and-bolts strategy. I presented myself as a Kickass Coach and talked about schedules and launches and formulas.

And once a client hired me, I did the real work—the soul-healing magic that allows the formulas to be successful. The clearing of negative energy, releasing of old beliefs, and reintegrating the lost and hidden parts, so women could be fully present and fully powerful in the world.

I NEVER talked about any of it.

My clients would say, "This is not what I expected."

And they came back over and over, purchasing package after package.

Now, something else was asking to be born through me ... something new and veiled.

Something so seductive and powerful that I found myself saying *yes. Yes. YES!*

At first, its presence was slow and tentative. The Feminine taking her time, unveiling.

By then, I was practiced at connecting with Source, at following the guidance of my Highest Self. Yet in many ways, I had cut her out of my business.

There had been no time to stop. To meditate. To unfurl.

It was go, go, go, all the time! I was doing what I needed to do to stay on track to earning six figures. Then fame. Then my rise to the level of the gurus.

That nudging I experienced that day was The Art of Feminine Marketing whispering her way in.

When I made space, I felt her. Her energy was bold, raspberry pink (and sometimes red), hot. She lit a fire in my womb and made my pussy tingle. She was flirtatious and powerful.

I committed to her right then.

And, we began to communicate.

She explained that she was part of a new paradigm of business—a new way of being that was *life giving* and *soul stirring*.

We got to know each other and her energy began to shine through me.

Old clients fell away. New ones took their place.

My income rose.

My programs changed. They became more soul centered.

While the nuts-and-bolts component remained, the connection to Source became a primary teaching.

I began hosting breakthrough retreats and invited soul-sisters to partner with me.

It wasn't easy. I was, at the time, pretty competitive and my inner gremlins would stress about all my clients leaving me for the magnificent women I was introducing them to.

But, The Art assured me that it was necessary—that collaboration was vital to women's success.

Today, those collaborators have become my closest friends. They are my web of support in the world. My teachers and confidants.

The Art collaborated with me to write a new manual, The Art of Feminine Marketing eBook. She guided me in designing marketing launches and new products. She told me how to tweak formulas to better suit my design.

She still lights me up when I feel tired, discouraged, and ready to quit. It is her energy that sustains me. That feeds my mission. That makes me show up even when I don't want to.

She is present now, here in this writing, dictating her story.

Here's the thing:

Your business is an energetic entity that needs YOU (a physical being) to birth it into the world. It is both a reflection of you, your gifts, your talents, your heart, AND of Source's desire for expansion in the world.

As such, it holds information you don't have.

It will guide you in choosing the right strategies, in tweaking formulas, and in designing its form in the physical realm.

Sounds pretty amazing, right? It is!

Now, it's time to start connecting with the Energy of Your Business.

Exercise: Connect with Your Business

**DOWNLOAD AN AUDIO VERSION OF THIS MEDITATION HERE: JULIEFOUCHT.COM/FMRESOURCES. **

Sit or lay comfortably in a place where you will not be disturbed for 20 minutes or more. Turn off any computer programs that might distract you with alerts. Switch your cell phone to silent. Turn off anything that might distract you from meeting with the Energy of Your Business. Have a journal and pen or word document open to record the details around your meeting after the meditation.

If you are adept at meditation and journaling, you may keep your fingers on your keyboard and transcribe your journey and conversation with the Energy of Your Business as it occurs.

Begin by closing your eyes and taking three deep breaths, moving the oxygen all the way down to your tailbone, feeling your spine lengthen, blowing the air all the way out through your nose. In and out. In and out. As you continue to breathe in and out, slow your breath and allow your body to soften, sinking into Mama Earth, who holds and nourishes us.

Now, turn your attention to the spot on your forehead between your eyes—your third eye. Notice this spot widening into a passageway that leads to the door of your private, secret garden—that place where only those you invite in and those who are there for your highest good can go.

As you enter the garden, notice what has changed or is different since the last time you were there.

Beneath your feet is a path that leads to the very center of the garden—the most sacred space. Follow the pathway into that sacred space. As you enter, notice the "helpers" who have gathered there for you … guides, guardian angels, and ancestors; all there for your highest good.

Now ask, "May I speak with the Energy of My Business?"

As the Energy of Your Business joins you, notice what it looks like and the shape it takes. How is it showing up? As light? Color? A piece of artwork? A creature or being?

Welcome the Energy of Your Business without judgment.

And now, you can begin asking your business questions.

Start with this one: "What do you need from me today?"

Listen without judgment to the answer your business provides. The answer may come in the form of the first words that pop into your mind, or as an image or feeling.

Next, ask your business if it is a good time to do some future planning. If you get a "yes" or "ok," here are some more questions you might ask:

- "Business, how would you like to grow?"

- "Business, what marketing strategies would you like me to use?"

- "Business, what is the next program or product you would like to birth?"

- "Business, what list-building strategies would you like me to launch?"

- "Business, what is the highest and best use of my time today?"

Finally, ask your business, "Business, what sign will you give me when I'm on the highest and best path for living my mission in the world?"

When you have completed your conversation with the Energy of your Business, thank it. Know that you can always come back to this place and speak with your business more.

Now, come fully back into your body. Feel the air on your skin and Mama Earth beneath your feet.

When you are ready, open your eyes, pick up your journal and record your conversation with the Energy of Your Business in detail.

Chapter 9
"THE WOUND IS THE PLACE THE LIGHT ENTERS US."

Rumi said, "The wound is the place where the light enters us."

Yet we tend to keep the wounded parts of ourselves hidden, locked away in darkness (even if we don't realize we're doing it).

We ALL have wounds—every single one of us.

And there is power hidden in them, if we are brave enough to look.

When you first come into the world, you remember your connection to Source and all that is. You've come from an unseen realm where all of your needs are met. You come to the world helpless, with the expectation that your needs will continue to be met.

As you enter the experiment of life, you experience wounding events, during which your needs are ignored, dismissed, or stomped on. When that happens, a part of you breaks off and slips into the shadows for protection.

Some wounds are experienced over and over, which then build into *beliefs*.

As adults, we rationalize our wounding experiences: *My mother couldn't hug me because she had a traumatic childhood.*

As children, though, we have yet to develop the capacity to *see outside ourselves*. So, the belief becomes about *us*. We have been wounded because there is something wrong with *us*.

As that belief is created, we unconsciously seek other experiences to bolster it. And, that's how it becomes the very thing that keeps us from living our highest and best life.

As love-based entrepreneurs, it keeps us from providing our best and deepest service to our clients (and often, from even offering that service in the first place).

This is why it's so important to crack the wound wide open! When we are willing to stand in the belief that has been created, the light enters. We no longer see the broken, defective person. We see the *pure soul*—the part of ourselves that is craving love and acceptance.

By looking directly at the wounded parts, healing happens.

Not only that, but the light we let in then becomes a magnet for others who share the same wounding beliefs! They are drawn to it. We attract those who need us most in *their* healing journey.

I spent a year working with Jeffery Van Dyk, founder of Tribal Marketing, to learn how to mine the gifts in wounds. His teachings center around how people develop a very particular and specialized set of skills that makes them uniquely qualified to serve a specific tribe as they navigate the wounding experiences of their life. He explains how healing your wounded parts makes you the perfect person to help heal those who have similar wounds.

It is not about having the right Facebook ads, or the best funnel in the world.

It is about who you BE—which in turn creates a mirror for those you are meant to serve, so they too can heal.

There is an exercise I do with some of my clients alongside one of my soul-sisters, Lindsay A. Miller. In it, I guide them in discovering the connection to the tribe the wound creates, the special skills the wound develops, and the words that will light the path for their "perfect" clients.

We bring women to abandoned parking lots/decaying buildings/the barren desert, and Lindsay photographs their wounds.

Here's what it looks like:

Day 1:

The women huddle together. They are giggly, nervous. The sky is grey, heavy with rain clouds. They are dressed strangely—one layered in the rags of homeless fashion, one in fishnet, one all in black with a hood covering her head, obscuring her face.

Ugly brown weeds crowd the cracks in the parking lot asphalt. Behind the women is an old restaurant, red and gold paint peeling from the walls. Broken flowerpots, an abandoned grocery cart, and old milk crates line one wall. It's the perfect backdrop for the work they are about to do.

A small, feral cat interrupts with persistent mewing. He thinks the women have come to feed him. We sense the others, hiding in dense shrubs beyond the edge of the parking lot. We feel their eyes upon us.

I know there will be other eyes throughout the day. Humans will be drawn to us. The women will not only experience what it means to be in their wounds, but they will also be seen in them, at their most vulnerable.

They will cry. They will curse at us. They will throw things and hide.

Cars will stop so drivers can stare. Some people will even approach us out of concern, interest, or pure curiosity to ask what we are doing.

The women will BE SEEN!

There is a moment in each shoot when the shift happens. The women in the group will have enough. Each will step into her own power. She will step into the truth—that she is *not* the ugly, stupid, worthless thing the belief has told her she is. That she is one with Source … a Divine Feminine beauty. That she has the power to create her life. That she has the responsibility to serve her clients, as she guides them out of the shadows of their own wounded beliefs.

And she knows she can do it, because she has now done it herself.

All of the emotions she felt during the photo shoot become the marketing language she uses to illuminate the path for the *right* clients to find her, because the feelings she experienced in the wound are the same feelings her tribe experiences … and the emotions she felt coming out of the wound are the emotions her tribe is craving.

These are the "away from" and "toward" motivators she will build into her marketing copy, her sales pages, her advertisements, etc.

Day 2:

We gather again the following day.

Lindsay has curated some of the best photos.

I feel my breath catch as she sets up her computer in front of the women.

There is silence around us.

My hands begin to tingle. I feel the energy rise as the hair on my arms stands up.

I sense all of the unseen helpers gathering, holding the space sacred.

Lindsay pushes the start button.

The photos slowly reveal themselves, one by one, woman by woman.

The wounded parts are seen, honored, and loved.

The women sigh as their pictures are shown. They cry. They feel love for this part of themselves that they have previously shamed and hidden.

They fall in love with themselves.

We fall in love with them.

They see the light that Rumi spoke of.

Chapter 10
THE WOUND RECOVERY PROCESS

When we are wounded, it hurts so much that we create strategies to avoid being wounded again. For many women, those strategies include putting on a polite mask and hiding the tender parts of ourselves. Pretending to be what we think is acceptable. Hiding who we really are.

But in order to attract our right clients, the ones we are meant to serve, we must have complete authenticity and magnetic marketing. We must take off the masks. This is what it means to be a love-based entrepreneur: to step fully out of the shadows and become visible, so those who need you can find you.

The reality is, so much marketing is shrouded in smoke and mirrors.

And it goes way back! From early childhood, when we enter school, we are taught the importance of getting all the answers right (or else).

The old masculine paradigm teaches us to "put on our game face" and be the "perfect" expert.

Guess what? Those behaviors teach us how to deny the wounded parts, the soft parts, the silly parts.

They create a wall of impenetrability.

But in today's social media-obsessed world, people crave intimacy and connection. They want to KNOW you before they buy from you.

So, you have to take down the wall.

You have to be willing to be vulnerable.

You have to share the imperfect.

You have to acknowledge the wound.

(OH SHIT. Right??)

I know … this is not the way we are taught.

The world teaches us to puff out our chest, to grab our chance, to push our way to the top, and to dominate.

The Art of Feminine Marketing teaches us differently.

She teaches us to be *all* of who we are—weak and strong. Wise and silly. Afraid and brave.

And through all of that, we attract clients, abundance, and joy with ease.

So, let's get started. It's time to reclaim the wounded parts of you!

Exercise: Discovering Your Wounds

Step 1: Create a timeline of your life. (You can print the one below or, re-create it on your own.) Think back to your earliest memory and begin noting any and all wounding experiences you can remember. No matter how big or small you might think the experience/wound was, take note of it. Give yourself an ample amount of time for this step. Don't rush it.

I've provided a sample to get you started—remember, you can download it here: **JULIEFOUCHT.COM/FMRESOURCES**.

Sample:

The Beginning: Pre-Birth to 18 Months	Wounds: When I was born, my parents hadn't chosen a girl's name. They wanted a boy. Finally, they named me after my mother. I didn't even deserve my own name. Beliefs: This happened to me because I am a disapointment/not what they wanted/defective.

The Early Years: 18 Months to 6 Years	Wounds: I sat on the curb waiting for Mom to come home from the neighbor's. I was all alone. Maybe five years old. Lonely and scared. I felt forgotten, unimportant. Beliefs: This happened to me because I am supposed to be self-sufficent. My longing is a sign that I'm weak, defective.
Elementary: 6 Years to 12 Years	Wounds: We moved to a new town. Mom sent me to play with the neighbors. They turned up the music, pretended they couldn't hear me. When I ran home in tears, Mom didn't believe me. Beliefs: This happened to me because I am unlikeable. My feelings don't matter. I'm defective for having them.
Early Teens: 12 Years to 15 Years	Wounds: Only one person came to my 13th birthday party. Mom tried to make it ok, but I wished she would just shut up. I was used to hiding my feelings by then ... used to not being important. Beliefs: This happened to me because I am not important/popular/pretty.

Late Teens: **15 Years to 19 Years**	Wounds: The hose came off the back of the toilet, causing water to flood the bathroom. I had no idea what was happening or how to fix it. I started bailing the water as I sent my little sister running across town to find Dad at a job. He came home and, instead of praising me for keeping the water out of the rest of the house with my bailing, was furious that I didn't just turn it off at the spout. I'm stunned, sad, crushed. How was I supposed to know about the spout? No one ever told me. Beliefs: This happened to me because I am defective. I can't do anything right.
Early Adulthood: **19 Years to 30 Years**	Wounds: Husband cheated on me. Beliefs: This happened to me because I am stupid, defective, and unworthy of being loved.

Step 2: Once you think you're finished creating your timeline, take a few deep breaths. Chances are high you're feeling a lot of emotions during and after that process. When you feel ready, it's time to revisit each wounding experience.

One by one, note the subconscious beliefs that were created to help explain why the particular wound happened to you.

**Remember: The belief is always about YOU. As adults, we can see the bigger picture. We can understand the way those who wounded us were first wounded themselves. As children, we don't have that insight. So, while you "unearth" the beliefs, ask, "If this was totally my fault, then it would happen because I am (fill in the blank)."

The first step in healing the belief is simply acknowledging it exists. We cannot heal that which we cannot see.

Your soul will know immediately that it is a false belief. It knows already that you aren't really stupid, or defective, or worthless, or any other word that comes up. And, just by doing this simple exercise, you may have already done the work to heal the belief.

As you write, you'll begin to see a pattern of similar beliefs. The same belief(s) tend to pop up over and over—the ones that form your core wounds. The clients who need you most will share similar ones.

And now, you understand your "perfect-for-you client" much more than you likely did before!

While you probably carry more than one false belief deep inside, there are one or two that carry the weight of all your decisions and struggles since your wounding. We call those "core beliefs," which can be as simple as the following examples:

I was born without a penis; therefore, I'm defective and unable to make my way in the world.

I am just a stupid, ugly, worthless girl.

When you discover the wound, treat yourself gently. You may want to fall sobbing to the ground (which is perfectly reasonable), but know that it's not really true. Give yourself plenty of love.

Printable Timeline—download it here: JULIEFOUCHT.COM/FMRESOURCES.

The Beginning: Pre-Birth to 18 Months	Wounds: Beliefs: This happened to me because I am…
The Early Years: 18 Months to 6 Years	Wounds: Beliefs: This happened to me because I am…
Elementary: 6 Years to 12 Years	Wounds: Beliefs: This happened to me because I am…
Early Teens: 12 Years to 15 Years	Wounds: Beliefs: This happened to me because I am…

Late Teens: 15 Years to 19 Years	Wounds:
	Beliefs: This happened to me because I am...
Early Adulthood: 19 Years to 30 Years	Wounds:
	Beliefs: This happened to me because I am...

My recurring core belief(s):

At this point, you have identified the core belief(s) that is/are holding you back from creating the business and life you crave.

The next step?

You *embody* the wound.

Exercise: Embodying the Wound(s)

Take your time preparing for and going through this particular exercise. It may require several hours to honor your wound, grieve it, and love it. The Feminine works at her own pace. You will get so much more out of this if you allow yourself the space and time to fully embrace your wound.

Set aside a notebook to record your emotions throughout the process. You may also consider inviting a trusted friend to be present, witness, and support you.

Step 1: Assemble your wound outfit. Pull items from your closet that represent you in your wound. Visit second-hand thrift stores and allow your intuition to pull items from the racks. Lay the clothes out on a bed or dresser, etc.

Step 2: Bless the space you are in. Ask that you be guided and guarded in this exercise—that the ancestors, guides, and angels who are supporting you in your highest good be present.

Step 3: Dress yourself in the clothes you've chosen. Take your time, noticing the details of the experience of transforming fully into the wound. Note the emotions that arise as you dress. Write them down using descriptive words.

Step 4: Allow yourself to sink fully into the wound. What does it feel like to be there? What does that part of you want and need?

Step 5: Observe yourself in a full-length mirror. Notice what you look like in the wound. How do you hold your body? What is expressed in your eyes? Allow any emotion that wants to rise to the surface. Welcome it and note it in your notebook.

Step 6: Open to receive love. Fill your heart with love by thinking about someone you love unconditionally: a child, niece or nephew, even a fur baby. Imagine that love has a color and a texture.

Now, look into your eyes in the mirror. Imagine you can open a door in your heart and allow all that love you feel for others to pour into the image you see of yourself in the mirror.

Love is one of those magical things that expands as you use it. So, the more love you pour into yourself, the more you will have for others.

Stay with the wound until you genuinely feel love toward that part of yourself. Notice what it feels like. What emotions come up now? Write those feelings in a separate column in your notebook.

Stay in this space of loving and feeling loved as long as you want.

Step 7: Revisit the words you used to describe what you were feeling as the wound. What emotions did you want to get away from? What did you long to feel instead? They will be the very "away from" and "toward" motivators you'll want to use in your marketing!

Chapter 11
CONNECTING WITH YOUR TRIBE

In the spirit realm, there is no time or distance.

It is a place where all things are possible and all dreams can come true. It is where we connect with Source—the all that is.

In this realm, it is possible to connect with the energy of those who carry the same wounding as you ... those you are meant to serve and help heal.

So, just as you connected with your Highest Self and the Energy of Your Business earlier to get to know them better, you can connect with the Energy of Your Perfect Client to understand him or her on a deeper level. You can also ask questions about what kind of programs s/he will purchase from you and what s/he will spend money on.

And as you spend time with your tribe on an energetic level, you will begin to understand them more deeply, and your marketing will speak more clearly to their hearts.

Exercise: Connect with the Energy of Your Perfect Tribe

**DOWNLOAD AN AUDIO VERSION OF THIS MEDITATION HERE: JULIEFOUCHT.COM/FMRESOURCES/. **

Sit or lay comfortably in a place where you will not be disturbed for 20 minutes or more. Turn off any computer programs that might distract you with alerts. Switch your cell phone to silent. Turn off anything that might distract you from meeting with the Energy of your Perfect Tribe. Have a journal and pen or word document open to record the details of your meeting after the meditation.

If you are adept at meditation and journaling, you may keep your fingers on your keyboard and transcribe your journey and conversation with the Energy of Your Perfect Tribe as it occurs.

Close your eyes and focus on your breath. Fill your belly with air and blow it out through your mouth. Breathe in and out, allowing the noise of the outside world to fade away.

Imagine you are standing in your private, secret garden where only you and those who are there for your highest good can enter.

Notice what has changed in the garden since you last visited. Notice the colors, the sounds, the scents.

Now you notice a pathway leading to the very center of the garden—the most sacred space where you are most connected to Source.

Follow the path into this sacred space.

Take a moment to look around at this space designed to perfectly support you.

There is a pile of beautiful polished stones, each the size of a dinosaur egg in one corner of the space. They are each a natural, vibrant color from Mama Earth, glowing in the light.

As you pick each one up, you notice a word etched into the stone. The words perfectly match your most important values. They might say *love, abundance, connection, justice* ... or any other values you hold.

Use the stones to outline a sacred circle in this space, placing each one with gratitude.

When the circle is done, step into the center. Open your heart and send a golden thread of love and invitation out into the world. You will feel a slight tug, as one of your tribemates captures the thread and sends you back one of his or her own.

Turn and send another thread, repeating the process.

Repeat again until you've turned a full 360 degrees, gathering all the threads that are sent back to you, thereby creating a beautiful map showing your people how to find you.

Now, ask for a representative of the tribe to step forward. This may be a person or a being who can speak for the whole tribe.

As the representative joins you, note what he or she looks like and how s/he carries him/herself.

Welcome that representative and thank him or her for being with you. Invite him or her to sit with you and have a conversation.

Here are some questions you might want to ask the representative of your tribe:

- Tribal Representative, tell me about the attributes of the tribe. What is your age range, relationship status, family status, income level, education level, attitude, beliefs, etc.?

- Tribal Representative, tell me about the biggest pain in your life and the life of the tribe. What are you crying about? What really sucks right now?

- Tribal Representative, tell me how I can help you solve that pain. What do you most want from me?

- Tribal Representative, tell me what you are willing to spend money on in order to solve this pain.

- Tribal Representative, tell me why you choose me to help you with this. What did I say or do?

- Tribal Representative, where did we find one another?

- Tribal Representative, what kind of program will be of the highest and best service to you?

♥ Tribal Representative, what would you most like me to include in the program or product I'm designing for you?

♥ Tribal Representative, is there anything else you want me to know?

Now, bring your conversation with your Tribal Representative to a close. Let him or her know how much you appreciate the sharing, and that you are available whenever s/he has more to share.

Allow the Tribal Representative to step back into the fabric of threads you collected. Lay the threads on the ground within the circle of stones, knowing they create the spiritual pathway for your people to find you. This circle will continue to live in your heart as you step back into the physical realm.

Come fully back into your body, now, feeling the air on your skin and the ground beneath your feet.

Pick up your journal and record everything you remember from this inner journey.

***Note: Use this meditation whenever you are creating a new program or launch, or whenever you might simply want to connect with your tribe energetically. Bonus tip: Send the heart invitations before you send marketing materials in the physical realm, so that the right people respond!

Love-Based Feminine Marketing:

Chapter 12
THE INNER SABOTEURS: RESISTANCE, PERFECTIONISM, INDECISION, OVERWHELM, AND PROCRASTINATION

I have a plan.

Today, I will write another 1500 words.

But it's Sunday, Resistance protests. *I want to rest, play, and watch movies on TV all day!*

I argue back, offering a compromise … *only 1000 words, then. Just one hour of writing.*

And then, here comes Overwhelm, shrieking, *We can't just do 1500 words today! I'll never get done! I have a freaking deadline. On weekdays I have clients, marketing, and new courses to create!*

Procrastination steps up to the plate. *But what about the cats? They haven't been bathed in weeks. They get baths, TODAY.*

I know these voices well. They are inner Saboteurs, and they keep me stuck. I recognize their power and their will to hold me in this place.

I've also heard some version of the same from every woman I've worked with over the last decade.

Your Saboteurs are the little voices in your head that insist you are "not ready, not skilled enough, not smart enough, not safe enough," etc. Their job in your psyche is to keep you safe. They do this by keeping you small, silent, and hidden. They urge against anything that would make you stand out powerfully.

Maybe you've heard this before. And maybe, you received this very common advice: "Feel the fear and do it anyway."

The problem is, that only works to a certain point, because constantly fighting against Fear is exhausting! It leads to burnout, illness, and eventually, giving up.

Saboteurs operate with a voice of authority. They know the exact right button to push with each woman to STOP her progress. They hide inside us like the engineers of some greater plan. "Not now, not yet, it's way too early, way too scary," they whisper.

There is a difference between listening to your Highest Self telling you to wait and germinate and listening to the gremlins of resistance, perfectionism, indecision, overwhelm, and procrastination.

You've felt them all before, right? Inside you? If so, you know they feel very different.

Saboteur energy feels limiting. It makes you shrink and hide. You may feel a block in your throat or your shoulders slump. The messages reflect the core wound of "not enoughness."

Messages from your Highest Self are expansive. They come from love. Your heart expands, your body vibrates, and you feel comforted in the expanse of possibility being crafted in you.

Saboteurs are tricky little beasts! Remember, they were originally designed to keep you safe, in response to an original core wound.

When we are children, we can't process the things that happen to us, so we create "Protectors" in our unconscious mind. These Protectors will do whatever they can to keep us safe. Some of their best strategies for doing so are to keep us hidden, to dim our light, to remind us not to speak out. They keep us small, so we become less of a target.

As we age, we become more capable of protecting ourselves and navigating the world safely. That's when our childhood Protectors morph into Saboteurs.

However, they *can* become helpful again … when we are able to connect with and care for the inner child part of ourselves. Because when we can keep him or her safe ourselves, we no longer need a Protector and the Saboteur simply melts away.

Oftentimes, you'll be able to recognize deeper fears within the Saboteurs.

Here's an example:

I drop into meditation.

My mind (Resistance) tries to pull me aside. "Don't look; don't write; don't go there."

Rather than push back, I simply notice.

A face appears in my meditation. A smooth, white mask (the kind shown in movie posters for horror flicks).

I'm instantly on guard.

"Who are you? Why are you here?" I ask.

"I am Fear," the mask responds.

"Why? I write all the time …" I say.

Fear tries the normal tactics—tapping in on the beliefs I have formed along the way. I might not be enough; my writing might be awful; my publisher might find out I'm a fraud.

None of it feels particularly heavy.

I soften. "Tell me more."

Fear sighs. "This is a tricky time," it says. "They are no longer hidden in the shadows. They are emboldened. Those that would keep The Feminine bound, that would lock her power in deep caves, that would bully and punish. They are here."

I realize that the old days of women being burned at the stake may not be as far away as I thought. Speaking out, speaking truth, speaking The Feminine magic may still be dangerous ... even deadly.

"But Fear," I whisper, "I still must speak."

I open my heart and begin to flow love into the mask.

It dissolves into a white mist that dissipates in the air, and I see, behind the fear, a little girl.

As the fear dissolves, I see all the places where I've asked my little inner girl to take charge. Gently, I ask her what she needs.

She tells me she needs to play in the sun, to walk in the hills behind my home, and play during the summer light.

I feel her lightness within me. I want to play, as well! So, I make a deal with her. This morning, I will write. Just 1000 words. She does not have to write any of them. She does not have to be present when my editor red lines the text. She does not have to help edit.

And then, when I am finished, we can play.

The little inner me smiles. She agrees happily and runs off to chase butterflies while I write.

Love-based entrepreneurs who practice The Art of Feminine Marketing know that *love and care are the path to ease and success.*

So, let's take a moment to work on whatever is standing in your way right now, in the form of resistance.

Exercise: Moving Past Resistance (Go here for the download: JULIEFOUCHT.COM/FMRESOURCES):

Think about something you are resisting in your business. It may be a project, a sales call, a launch, etc.

Step 1: Fill in the following with it in mind. (You can do this in your journal, as well.)

I am resistant about completing:

As you think about this, notice what emotions arise. What are you *feeling*?

This makes me feel:

Notice where in your body you feel this emotion. Allow the emotion to become even stronger.

I feel this in my:

Notice if the emotion has a shape. Does it take the form of a being? Or does it show up as an energy or color? Focus your energy on the emotion, making it clear.

This emotion shows up as:

Step 2: Now, thank the emotion for being with you—for all the ways it has tried to keep you safe.

Then, open your heart and begin to pour love into that emotion. Keep pouring until the emotion is completely brimming over with your love.

Notice the part of you that was hiding behind the emotion before. How old is that part of you? How is she dressed? What is her emotional state? (Write your answers down.)

Step 3: Imagine standing or kneeling in front of your inner child. Take her hands in yours and look deeply into her eyes. Tell her you are so sorry for everything she has been through that has made her afraid. Let her know she is no longer responsible for the work she is incapable of doing. The adult you will now take over.

Ask this part of you what she needs from you. She may want more hugs, more love, or more play time.

Remember, the child part of us doesn't get to be in charge. But she deserves to have her needs for love and security met. You, as the adult, now have the privilege of caring for and healing your own inner little girl.

Step 4: Finally, invite your Highest Self to join you. Ask if there is anything else that needs to be addressed before you go back to your project.

Chapter 13
CARING FOR THE VESSEL

In the exercises you've completed so far, you've connected with your Highest Self—your representation of The Divine Feminine. You've spoken with the Energy of Your Business and the Energy of Your Perfect Tribe, dissolved inner Saboteurs, and loved and cared for your inner child.

You've become versed in moving in the spirit world!

You *are* a spiritual being in a physical body.

Now, it's time to talk about your body—an incredibly important tool in your success toolkit that isn't talked about nearly enough.

We receive all kinds of messages from society about our bodies and physical appearance. We should look like supermodels (who never eat). We should spend thousands of dollars on products to keep our faces line free. We should carve out two hours a day to go to the gym. We should only ever drink beer and eat nachos on the weekends. We should join weight watchers. We should curl or straighten our hair.

All of these messages convey to us one single point: we are not good enough. We are not pretty enough. We are not the right shape, color, or age.

These messages cause us to ignore the real needs of our body.

Oddly enough, we are never taught to actually stop and listen to our body—the vessel that carries us through the world. The vehicle that allows us to do our work.

The truth is, we need strength and stamina to keep going. Not in a "push through" kind of way, but in a "dipping-into-natural-reserves" way that is possible when we honor and care for our body.

The reality is, your body can be one of your most valuable allies, or it can take you out of the game completely.

Years and years ago, I met a woman named Mary Kay. Mary Kay had breast cancer. Her goal was to live long enough to see her son graduate high school.

She was the sweetest, nicest person.

And then she died.

Two days after her death, my then mother-in-law told me about a dream she had. In the dream, Mary Kay came to her and said, "I thought I needed to be nice to people. But my body wanted me to be real. And, when I refused to be real, my body couldn't take the dichotomy. It took me out."

I often wonder what would've happened if Mary Kay had been able to speak with her body—if she had been able to receive a message from it before she died.

This is a very dramatic example of the importance of listening to your body's wisdom. I see this same type of thing over and over in my clients' lives (and in my own, in less dramatic ways).

To be honest, this is the area where I struggle the most. I would much rather write a marketing email then go to the gym! Yet my body no longer allows me to slack on my self-care.

I've learned to listen when my body speaks, and to seek out its wisdom. Rather than follow the latest diet craze, I listen to what it tells me it needs. Now, my emotions might say, "ice cream," but my body tells the truth! "I need yams and leafy greens today," it might say. Or "I need to move ... to dance and swing my arms."

When I fail to listen, I suffer.

Learning to tap into your body's wisdom and allow it to guide you in caring for your vessel is the next step in the Art of Feminine Marketing.

Just like in previous meditations, there is a spiritual part of you that represents your physical body. I like to call her "the Body Singer." She will let you know when you need to rest, when you need to dance, and when you need to bring more physical pleasure into your life. In other words, she will tell you how to tune the body instrument to optimal performance!

Exercise: Connect with Your Body Singer

**DOWNLOAD AN AUDIO VERSION OF THIS MEDITATION HERE: JULIEFOUCHT.COM/FMRESOURCES. **

Sit or lay comfortably in a place where you will not be disturbed for 20 minutes or more. Turn off any computer programs that might distract you with alerts. Switch your cell phone to silent. Turn off anything that might distract you from meeting with the energy of your Body Singer. Have a journal and pen or word document open to record the details of your meeting after the meditation.

If you are adept at meditation and journaling, you may keep your fingers on your keyboard and transcribe your journey and conversation with your Body Singer as it occurs.

Close your eyes and focus on your breath. Fill your belly with air and blow it out through your mouth. Breathe in and out, allowing the noise of the outside world to fade away.

Imagine you are standing in your private, secret garden where only you and those who are there for your highest good can enter.

Notice what has changed in the garden since you last visited. Notice the colors, the sounds, the scents.

Now, notice a pathway leading to the very center of the garden—the most sacred space where you are most connected to Source.

Follow the path into this sacred space.

Take a moment to look around at this space designed to perfectly support you.

Ask, "May I speak with the representative of my physical body, my Body Singer?"

As she appears, note what she looks like, what she is wearing, what her energy feels like.

Thank her for joining you and settle in for a chat.

Ask her:

- What does my body want me to know?

- Are there any specific concerns I should be paying attention to?

- What does my body want me to do today to support it?

- Are there any foods I should eliminate or add more of to my diet?

- What else does my body need?

- What sign will you give me when I need to stop and pay attention to the messages of my body?

When you have completed your conversation with your Body Singer, thank her. Make an appointment to come back and speak with her again soon.

Now, come fully back into your body. Feel the air on your skin, and Mama Earth beneath your feet.

When you are ready, open your eyes, pick up your journal, and record your conversation with your Body Singer in detail.

Chapter 14
CREATING YOUR INNER MASTERMIND

I feel them as I enter the room.

First, my own spirit guides—the Native American grandfather takes the north corner. In the east, Dell, the tall, thin spirit who ensures I'm connected to my beloved. Behind him stands the archangel Michael, with a sword of truth. Gathered in the South corner are the Grandmothers, led by my strong, adventurous Grandma Cornwall. And in the west are the three witches—parts of me reclaimed from past lives. I see they have brought a pot ... a symbol, they say, of the magic we are about to create.

They are all silent witnesses of the work I'm doing to change things for our future.

I welcome them and thank them for being here. I ask that they create a safe space for the women who will join us: "Guide us and guard us for the best and highest good of all," I say.

They agree.

Then I feel the others—the inner counsel of women who will join this gathering. Some are known to the women; some have been guiding for years without notice or acknowledgement.

They fill the room: the fairies, the star people, the dragons. I'm honored by their presence and I know it is going to be one amazing event!

We are born to human mothers and fathers as babies in human form. Yet we are also spirits, filling a body in this life for a particular purpose. We belong to a spirit family, just as we belong to a human family. There are spirits who choose to follow us into this life to guard us and guide us. They have a view of us from the spiritual plane.

In literature, we often see them show up as fairy godmothers or guardian angels.

They are powerful allies on your journey.

However, they sometimes don't understand the limits of the human body. They must be brought into communication with those parts of you in order to understand. When joined together with your Highest Self, the Energy of Your Business, and your Body Singer, they create a powerful inner counsel.

And assembling your counsel is the final inner piece in need of completion before you begin creating your marketing plan!

Exercise: Assembling Your Inner Mastermind Counsel

**DOWNLOAD AN AUDIO VERSION OF THIS MEDITATION HERE: <u>JULIEFOUCHT.COM/FMRESOURCES</u>. **

Sit or lay comfortably in a place where you will not be disturbed for 20 minutes or more. Turn off any computer programs that might distract you with alerts. Switch your cell phone to silent. Turn off anything that might distract you from meeting with your Mastermind Council. Have a journal and pen or word document open to record the details of your meeting after the meditation.

If you are adept at meditation and journaling, you may keep your fingers on your keyboard and transcribe your journey and conversation with your Mastermind Counsel as it occurs.

Close your eyes and take a deep breath in. Slowly let it out, bringing your attention inward. Breathe in again, feeling the air fill your body with life-sustaining oxygen. Blow the air all the way out of your body through your mouth. Notice how the outside noise fades away, allowing you to more deeply enter this quiet and calm inner realm. Breathe in again, welcoming love and healing into your body. Blow out all the stress and negativity that clings to you.

As you continue to breathe in and out, imagine you are standing in your secret, private garden. This is a sacred space where only you and those entities who are there for your highest good can enter.

Take a few moments to explore. Notice the type of plants, the sun or moonlight. Are there any animals or magical beings in your garden? What are you feeling as you explore?

Now, notice the path in front of you. Follow it as it guides you deeper and deeper into the very center of the garden—the most sacred place where you are most strongly connected to Source.

As you enter the center of your garden, take a moment to look around.

Notice that some kind of boardroom table or gathering place has grown in your garden. There is exactly the right number of chairs for your perfect inner council, in exactly the right shape for each entity that will be joining you.

One at a time, the members of your mastermind council enter.

First, your Highest Self. Greet her and thank her for being there to support you.

Second, your Body Singer. Thank her for taking care of your physical vehicle and being there.

Following her is the Energy of Your Business. Celebrate that your business is there, and thank it for joining you.

Next, your Tribal Representative. Thank her for showing up on behalf of your tribe.

Finally, other entities and energies who are present for your highest and best good (and that of your tribe) enter. Greet each one, noting their roles, and thanking them for being present.

Now, take a seat at the table.

For this first meeting of your mastermind, you might want to share your vision and dreams, allowing members to offer their ideas and add to the vibrancy of your vision.

When everyone has had a chance to speak, thank them for attending and set a date for your next meeting. Let them know how valuable their input is.

Close the meeting. Walk back up the path, beginning to notice your breath as you breathe in and out, in and out. Feel the air on your skin and the ground beneath your feet as you come fully back into your body, fully present, as if you've had the perfect amount of rest.

Record this experience in your journal or in a word document.

Open your calendar and reserve time for your next mastermind council meeting. **Keep this appointment with your inner council sacred! They are vital to a business that is birthed from your own inner knowing, connected to Source, and profitable. Check in OFTEN!

Finally, set aside time to create a visual representation of the vision you and the mastermind created.

**Bonus tip: Pinterest has some great vision maps. You can also use poster board and pictures cut from magazines, or any other visual medium that works for you.

Love-Based Feminine Marketing:

Chapter 15
THE DANCE OF THE FEMININE AND THE MASCULINE

Each of us embodies both Divine Masculine and Divine Feminine energy. When they are aligned, magic happens! New ideas, thought leadership, and extraordinarily unique and applicable solutions appear.

As The Feminine plays in the spirit realm, spinning new programs, products, and answers, a natural energy builds. The Divine Masculine uses this energy to take action, manifesting the dreams of The Feminine on the physical plane.

If we stay too much in The Feminine, going inward, connecting, and never bringing our vision into the world, we fail the people we are meant to serve. They are left with the pain you are meant to help them heal. They are left, as my friend Therese says, "crying in the darkness for you."

On the other hand, if we are too much in The Masculine, constantly pushing forward, we fail to sink into the deeper work. For many women, this results in exhaustion, adrenal fatigue, and life-threatening illness.

I know too many women who have built successful six- and seven-figure businesses only to fall ill or fall out of love with the work. Then, it becomes drudgery.

Brave hearts choose to start over and create from the new paradigm of Feminine Marketing.

In the first half of this book, I shared stories and exercises to help you connect with your Divine Feminine, to seek guidance from the energy of your right tribe, and to heal the inner parts that hold you back.

Now that you know who your tribe is, it is time to lay a trail of breadcrumbs in the physical world, so they can find you. (Don't worry, you're going to be checking in with the Energy of Your Business along the way, to make sure you stay on the right path.)

I'm going to outline four basic strategies. Then, you will have a conversation with the Energy of Your Business to customize each strategy to your unique skill set. From there, you'll create a custom marketing plan that brings you joy, attracts the right people, and feels like paddling downstream!

Here are the four strategies:

- Warm Market Reach-Out Calls
- Face to Face
- Content Marketing
- Establishing Expertise from the Stage

1. Warm Market Reach-Out Calls

These calls are designed to connect with people you already know and invite them into a deeper conversation about what you are up to and how it might benefit them (or someone they know).

2. Face to Face

Here, you create a plan for meeting new people, and for determining whether they are part of your tribe. If they are, you'll invite them into a deeper conversation about how you can serve them.

3. Content Marketing

You'll create a plan for sending "love letters" to your tribe in the form of free gifts, blog posts, newsletters, social media posts, videos, podcasts, and/or social media Lives. This is a courtship based on providing value that will lead to sales down the road (or right away).

4. Establishing Expertise from the Stage

When you step onto the stage as a "featured speaker," you have automatic credibility. It also spreads your message to a wider audience, exponentially increasing your influence in the world. (Don't worry—while this is really scary for many, we'll work with your Highest Self to make it fun and profitable!)

All four of these client-generating activities result in the following outcomes:

Love-Based Feminine Marketing:

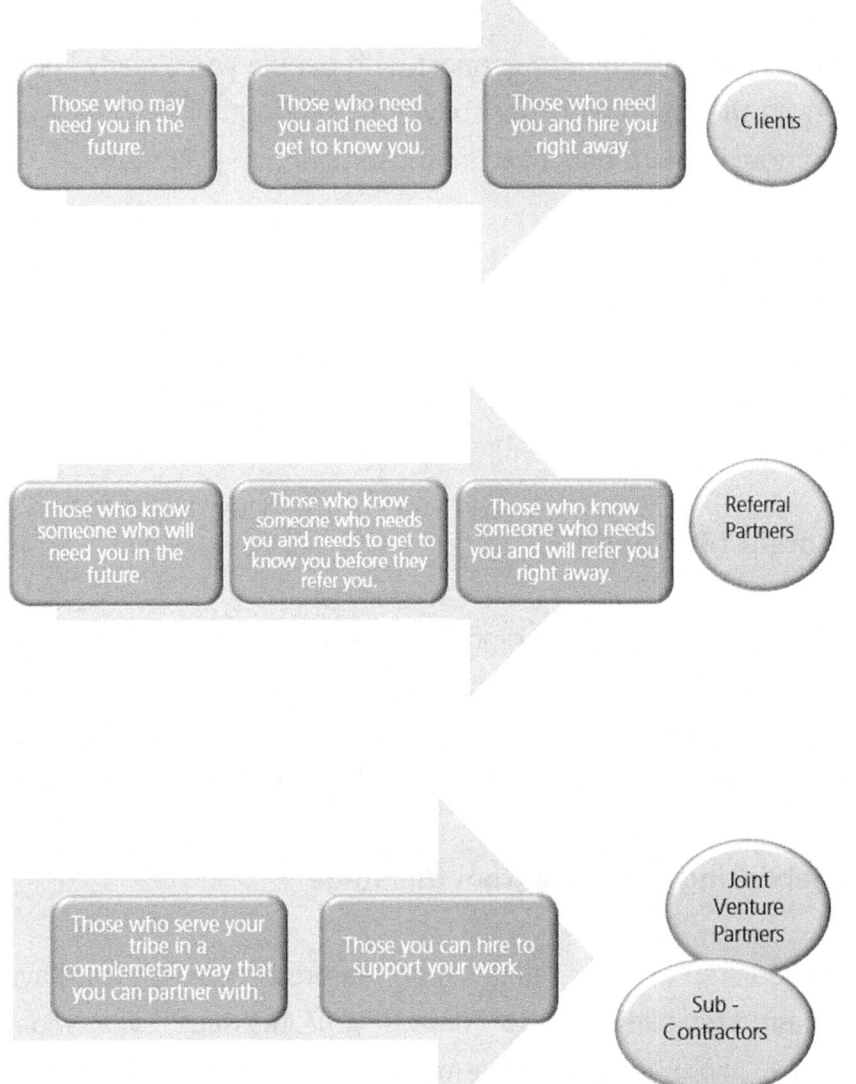

It's time to dive into the four strategies! Each one is solid marketing. Each will help you grow. And, each becomes brilliant only when you put your own twist on it by evoking the wisdom of your deeper knowing, your connection to source, and the sometimes-hidden parts of yourself.

Chapter 16
MARKETING STRATEGY 1: WARM MARKET REACH-OUT ... THE FEMININE WAY

Get out that journal and pen again ... it's time to prepare for warm market reach-out calls!

Exercise: Warm Market Reach-Out Calls

Step 1: Make your lists. Make a list of everyone you know in your tribe demographic—you might title it, "My Tribe."

Now, don't be surprised if your inner Saboteurs come out swinging in order to stall this process! They might whisper about all the negative, terrible, disastrous, and even deadly things that can happen when you step into public eye.

They might urge you to stay in the shadows, in the hopes that someone will find you naturally. (After all, you do spend a lot of time posting pictures of your cat on Instagram. Okay ... maybe that's just me!)

If this happens, stop what you are doing and go back to the process outlined in Chapter 12 for moving past resistance. Dissolve your Saboteur with love and care for your inner child.

Then, come back to making your list.

This is perfect work for your mind. Your mind was designed to gather, sort, and store data. It has an amazing filing system you can use to make your list.

The average person knows thousands of people by name. Not all of those people will be in your niche. As a matter of fact, most won't. Do it anyway!

Challenge yourself to create a list of 100 names. Going beyond the easy and comfortable five or 10 or even 20 will flip a switch. You'll "unbox" the files in your head, and names will pop up that you wouldn't have thought of if you hadn't been pushing for 100.

NOTE: YOU WILL NOT BE CALLING EVERYONE ON THE LIST.

So, relax and just make it.

At the same time, you might notice names popping out that are NOT your ideal tribe. Great Uncle John is wonderful (at least mine is!), but he isn't ever going to be a member of The Art of Feminine Marketing Community.

However, he might know someone who could.

So, start a second list of potential referral partners. Add the names of colleagues who do work that would be beneficial to your tribe.

Now, traditional marketing would dictate that you leave those who do the same thing you do off this list. This is scarcity thinking. "They will take my clients if I let them. They will steal my profits."

The Art of Feminine Marketing is all about abundance. Notice the difference in thinking: "Source provides for me. So, if someone is meant to be my client, she will choose me. If she would be better served by someone else, then someone better will come along for me. Source takes care of me, making sure all my needs are met."

When you fully trust in Source and the abundance of the universe, there is no reason to avoid those who do similar work. Not only do you have more power together, but ultimately, determining who will be best served by each of you is the greatest way to honor those we serve.

So, go ahead and add them to your Potential Referral Partner List.

Next, add phone numbers and emails to the lists for each person.

Step 2: Engage your body compass. Your body is the most beautiful, amazing compass available to provide you with direction. Unfortunately, society teaches us to ignore our body's wisdom in favor of idolizing the altar of the intellect. We are told to analyze and to make decisions based on logic.

Learning to listen to and trust your body's guidance is a priceless tool in creating a dream business and life.

Imagine you have the most delicious food in front of you. This is one of your favorite things to eat. How does your body respond? Do you lean forward toward the food? Perhaps your lips curl into a smile. Maybe you take a deep breath and your shoulders relax.

Now, imagine that plate is taken away, replaced with something you detest. Notice again how your body reacts. You might wrinkle your nose, tighten your lips, and/or lean backward.

These are your body's natural signals for indicating a "YES!" and "NO WAY!"

So, this next step is about using your body as a yes/no compass for your lists.

Go through the list, read each name, close your eyes, and notice how your body reacts.

Put a star next to each name that feels like a "yes."

Voila! You've just made your first marketing list!

Come back to this list monthly to add names and repeat the compass process. People who were formerly "NO WAY"s may, over time, become "YES"s. Things change, and so might their needs and openness.

Step 3: Make a spiritual connection. Settle into your meditation space. Open a word document or your journal, so you can take notes during this process.

**DOWNLOAD AN AUDIO VERSION OF THIS MEDITATION HERE: JULIEFOUCHT.COM/FMRESOURCES. **

We're going to use the same meditation here as we did in Chapter 7 to get you to your sacred garden.

Close your eyes and take a deep breath in. Let it out slowly, bringing your attention inward. Breathe in again, feeling the air fill your body with life-sustaining oxygen. Blow the air all the way out of your body through your mouth. Let outside noise fade away, allowing you to more deeply enter the inner realm. Breathe in again, welcoming love and healing into your body, blowing out all the stress and negativity that clings to you as you exhale.

As you continue to breathe in and out, imagine you are standing on a beach. Notice what the waves look like, what color the water is. Notice the feel of the air on your skin and the sounds of the beach around you.

Now, notice a door, standing all by itself, on the beach. Nothing behind it, nothing in front. Just a door.

What color is the door? What is it made of? Notice the doorknob. What is its color and shape?

In a moment, you are going to go through the door into your own secret, private garden. This is a sacred space where only you and those entities who are there for your highest good can enter.

Open the door and step into your garden.

Take a few moments to explore. Notice the types of plants, the sun or moonlight. Are there any animals or magical beings in your garden? What are you feeling as you explore?

Now, notice the path in front of you. Follow it as it guides you deeper and deeper into the very center of the garden—the most sacred place where you are most strongly connected to Source.

Ask your Highest Self to join you.

When she does, thank her for her wisdom and for always being there for you. Then ask, "Who, on the list, should I reach out to this week? Can you give me the names of five people who would be ideal for me to speak to?"

Listen and note who she advises.

One by one, ask to speak with the Highest Self of those she has named.

Ask them, "What is the highest and best use of my call to you? What do you need to hear from me? How can I best serve you?"

Record their answers.

(Alternatively, you can have a conversation with the first person on the list, thank him or her, end the meditation, and make the phone call. You can then come back to the meditation before reaching out to the next person on the list, and so on.)

Close the meditation, thanking all who were present. Feel the energy and spirit of your Highest Self, who lives within and is part of you.

Come fully back into your body, feeling the air on your skin and the ground beneath your feet.

Step 4: Dial!! Block out time in your calendar to make your reach-out calls. Treat this as you would any other appointment. This is not something to be put off or canceled because you didn't feel like it/ the cat wanted your attention/someone asked you to help them rearrange their furniture. Keeping this appointment with yourself is a boundary-setting exercise that will prove indispensable as your business grows, and more and more people want your time.

Now, before you dial, script your call.

If its someone you know well, you can start by saying something like, "You know that I've been in a certification to (fill in your expertise here). Are you open to booking time to chat about (fill in what their Highest Self said they most wanted)?"

Assure the person you're speaking with that it's a no-obligation conversation and that, while her name popped up for you, you are only looking for a right match. The conversation is to find out if you are right to help her solve her pain—*not* to talk her into anything.

Allow her to answer. If you get a "no," thank her and ask if she knows of anyone who might want an exploratory conversation.

If you get a "yes," open your calendar and suggest two different times that work for you for the exploratory conversation. Schedule a date and time right then.

If it's someone you haven't talked to for a while, acknowledge that.

You might say, "I know it's been a while since we talked. Your name keeps popping up in my head. I want to get caught up, and I want to share a little bit about what I'm up to. Would that be ok?"

Be genuinely interested in what he or she shares.

Allow your body compass to guide you. Take notes so you know what you asked, what info the connection gave you, and what info you didn't find out this time so you know how to follow up.

Step 5: Track your numbers. Create a tracking sheet, so you know how many people you talked to in order to schedule one exploratory call, and how many exploratory calls you had to get one new client to commit to working with you. This information will come in handy when you strategize later for bigger launches.

Step 6: Tweak your strategy. As you experiment with this strategy, notice what works for you and what doesn't. Convene your Inner Mastermind, your Highest Self, the Energy of Your Business, your Tribal Representative, and any other spirit guides, angels, and ancestors who are there for your highest good. Ask them to give their viewpoint on this strategy.

Then, practice it. Get comfortable with it and make it yours!

Love-Based Feminine Marketing:

Chapter 17
MARKETING STRATEGY 2: FACE TO FACE

Every time I walk into a new networking group, I feel nervous. The little seven-year-old child in me starts to fret.

When I was seven, my family moved from the only home I'd ever known. In my old neighborhood, I was uber-confident. I was the president of our Girls-Only Club because the clubhouse was in my yard. I was the director of our neighborhood talent shows because I created the scripts.

When a girl from down the street confronted me one day, asking why I got to be in charge, I replied (in utter shock), "Because … ummm."

It had never occurred to me that I wouldn't be!

Then, we moved to the haunted house in the mountains where my parents spent their summer months as kids, and where they met. It was a second home to them. But suddenly, I was an outsider.

For the first time, I was excluded from play circles. And, when I ran home and cried to my mother, I was told I was being "too sensitive." Surely, those kids didn't mean what I'd heard. Then I was sent upstairs to my room, where the ghosts (who were unhappy with me) were.

Each time I walk into a new networking group, my little seven-year-old self remembers trying to break into the circle of kids in that new community. She remembers feeling so alone and unimportant. She remembers the rejection of not being believed. She remembers the terror the ghosts stirred in her.

It used to be almost unbearable.

But I do it anyway. Because my mission depends on it! And, that lights a fire within that is stronger than the fear of my seven-year-old me.

Today, I have the tools to calm her. To care for her before I enter a room, so she feels safe and loved. (If you've read the first half of this book, you now have those tools, as well.)

And I've learned something along the way: I will be welcomed with open arms. Each group holds the promise of new clients, new partners, and new bff's. (This book itself would not exist if I had chosen to stay home and not attend an event, because it was there that I met my amazing publisher!)

Face-to-face marketing, or networking, is all about weaving webs of connection to support and inspire. One of the biggest traps of networking groups is that they become competitive, limiting the number of members in each profession … even pulling down members who begin to rise above others in success.

And, if you aren't careful, it's easy to get sucked into that crab pot of jealousy.

So, as you network the Feminine Way, you keep your heart tethered to Source, aware of the abundance that is the basis of all life, that wants only the best for you. You'll bring a different energy into your networking experiences and you'll experience amazing results!

Any face-to-face event can be broken into three separate phases: the pre-party prep, walking the red carpet, and the after party.

Exercise: Face-to-Face Marketing

Pre-Party Prep

During your pre-party prep, you scope out where your tribe hangs out, set your intention for networking, and make sure you are coming from a happy mindset.

Step 1: Find out where your tribe hangs out.

You've already done the work to identify your tribe. You've discovered how to best serve them. You know what their big pain is.

Now, it's time to complete a simple online search. For instance, if you serve businesswomen, you might search "businesswomen organizations and associations" in your town. If your tribe consists of moms with preschoolers, type that into your web browser. Note any organizations or meetings that show up.

Next, subscribe to www.meetup.com. You'll be asked to choose the types of events you would like to be notified about. Choose the ones that fit your tribe, and just like that, you'll receive regular updates of related events in your area.

Ask your current clients, business associates, and friends (both online and offline) for referrals to organizations that hold events where your tribe hangs out.

Get creative! Most likely, your tribe consists of people just like you. So, where do *you* hang out? The gym, PTA meetings, in church groups, at the roller rink? Are your tribe members likely to attend Chamber of Commerce events, city council meetings, or community volunteer activities? Be creative in your search and note additional events where you might run into your perfect client.

Next, expand your search to one-time or yearly events in your area that might attract your tribe. While you might not want to attend multi-day events all the time, they are great places to meet people and develop deep relationships quickly.

Finally, check in with your Inner Mastermind. Are there places you've overlooked or didn't know about?

List the organizations/associations and events you discover.

Finally, research the most likely organizations or groups on your list to determine their meeting dates, times, locations, and costs.

Step 2: Engage your body compass.

Just as you used your body to guide you in choosing who to reach out to in the warm marketing exercise, you'll use your body to choose which events to attend each month.

Read the list you've created. For each one, ask, "Is this an optimal event?" Feel which way your body leans. As you get more adept at this practice, refine the responses you receive. They may come with sounds, or a feeling of peace and clarity. Notice how your body works and lean into its knowing.

Choose three to five events to attend each month. If you find a "rich vein" (a group with a lot of your tribe members), continue to check in with your body and your Inner Mastermind to assure it continues to serve your highest and best good, and that of your tribe.

Calendar the events you plan to attend. Like any appointment, these are non-negotiable once they are on your calendar. Unless you or a family member is deathly ill, make the commitment to yourself and your business to attend.

Step 3: Set your intention.

What do you want to achieve from your networking? How many new people do you want to connect with? Intention requires that you be very, very specific, so this is not the place to fudge your numbers or to speak in generics, like, "as many as possible."

You wouldn't tell a waiter to just bring you something you'll love to eat, right? So why approach your business with a "whatever-shows-up-is-fine" attitude?

For each event, note the number of new contacts you intend to make. Imagine walking through your door after the event with a handful of new phone numbers. Tap into how you will feel.

Step 4: Check your supplies.

Make sure you have all of the following before you show up:

- 💚 A pocketful of business cards. (Note: Do not let a lack of business cards prevent you from heading out to an event. No one buys because of business cards. No one decides not to buy because of a lack of cards. They are just little rectangles of paper. Who you BE is much more important.)

- 💚 A notebook and pen to write down contact info for people who don't have a business card to give you.

- 💚 Your phone or calendar to schedule complimentary sales calls on the spot.

Step 5: Send a spiritual invite.

It's time to go inside and prepare your spiritual path, *before you walk out the door.*

**DOWNLOAD AN AUDIO VERSION OF THIS MEDITATION HERE: JULIEFOUCHT.COM/FMRESOURCES. **

Sit or lay comfortably in a place where you will not be disturbed for 20 minutes or more. Turn off any computer programs that might distract you with alerts. Switch your cell phone to silent. Turn off anything that might distract you from meeting with the Energy of your Perfect Tribe. Have a journal and pen or word document open to record the details of your meeting after the meditation.

If you are adept at meditation and journaling, you may keep your fingers on your keyboard and transcribe your journey as it occurs.

Close your eyes and focus on your breath. Fill your belly with air and blow it out through your mouth. Breathe in and out, allowing the noise of the outside world to fade away.

Imagine you are standing in your private, secret garden where only you and those who are there for your highest good can enter.

Notice what has changed in the garden since you last visited. Notice the colors, the sounds, the scents.

Now, you notice a pathway leading to the very center of the garden—the most sacred space where you are most connected to Source.

Follow the path into this sacred space.

Take a moment to look around at this space designed to perfectly support you.

There is a pile of beautiful polished stones, each the size of a dinosaur egg in one corner of the space. They are each a natural, vibrant color from Mama Earth, glowing in the light.

As you pick each one up, you notice a word etched into the stone. The words perfectly match your most important values. They might say *love, abundance, connection, justice* ... or any other values that you hold.

Use the stones to outline a sacred circle in this space, placing each stone with gratitude.

When the circle is done, step into it.

Send cords of love and invitation into the world and feel the pull of response from a tribemate.

Turn, send another cord, and feel the response. Turn again.

Continue circling until you have turned 360 degrees. Gather all the threads sent back to you, notice how beautiful each is on its own, and when woven together in a community tapestry.

Tuck your tapestry in a safe place in your heart to carry with you into the networking event.

Step 6: Check your mindset.

You've done your prep work. You've set your intention.

Now, let it go!

Allow Source to take over and do its part. Your job is to show up and be happy.

Say to yourself, "I'm going to this event and I am going to have fun." Let go of any self-criticism or fear. Fill your body with love, putting your inner Saboteur to sleep. And, just have fun!

Step 7: Walk the Red Carpet.

Walking the red carpet is all about showing up fully—no more hiding out by the snack table! It includes how you'll approach new people with ease, and how to have the best conversation the other person has ever had.

I remember reading a sociological study when I was still in college. A bunch of college students boarded an airplane and sat next to complete strangers. They were instructed not to tell the strangers anything about themselves (not even their names). They simply asked questions and were very, very interested in learning all about the stranger.

Upon exiting, the strangers were asked to comment on the person they sat next to on the airplane. Every single one of them said that the person was the most interesting they had *ever* met.

And they couldn't even tell the interviewer the person's name!

To become the most interesting person in the room, get genuinely, lovingly curious about other people.

How to start a conversation:

1. **Imagine going to a fun cocktail party.** The worst thing possible is for you to ambush people with all the details of your business immediately upon meeting them, right? Remember the 80/20 rule: 80% of the conversation should be about them and 20% about you.

2. **Be your brand.** Show up ready to represent your business in its best light. Connect with your Highest Self just before you walk through the door and allow her to shine through you.

3. **Look for individuals who are sitting or standing alone and approach them with a smile.** Make it your goal to help them feel comfortable. Hold out your hand and introduce yourself. Wait for them to introduce themselves and ask how long they've been part of the group. Be of service to them.

4. **Look for groups that are open,** allowing you space to slip in, versus the tight little circles whispering together. Approach with a smile and wait for the group to shift allowing you space. This happens automatically in most situations. Again, hold out your hand and say, "Hi."

5. **Find something to compliment the person on.** Women love to hear that their new blouse is just fabulous, or that the shoes they're wearing are really cute.

6. **Be quiet and get really curious.** Truly listen to what the person has to say. Ask questions. Be present to what the other person is saying versus being in your head, thinking about how you will respond.

7. After a few minutes, **thank the person for his or her time,** and suggest that you both go meet other people. Express how much you enjoyed talking and ask for a card so you can continue the conversation. You can book a time to talk later before you part, if appropriate. If it's someone new to the group, don't abandon her! Introduce her to someone you know in the group, and then move on.

The After Party

Ahh, this is where many entrepreneurs fail. They take the stack of business cards they've collected and file them away, never to be seen again! Instead, let's turn those contacts into clients and profit.

So, what's the first thing you should do after returning from a networking event? Open wine? No (as tempting as it might be!).

Step 1: Write in your gratitude journal.

The very first thing you should do is to *record three good things* that happened at the event in your gratitude journal. This will create neural pathways that fire good feelings toward networking in the future. Gratitude is an easy and necessary wealth principal.

Step 2: BRAG!

We are taught as children (especially as girls) NOT to brag. We are to be modest. But bragging is actually an excellent way to create deep rhythms of success. Review your evening, noting what you did that you are most proud of. If you've got a trusted friend, partner, or mastermind group, brag to him or her. If not, brag in the mirror.

Fully embracing the brag, say, "I brag that I …"

What we focus on, we attract more of. Most people focus on what they *didn't* do well and get more of that. So, by focusing on what you *did* do well, you will attract more of what you want.

Step 3: Within 24 hours, sort the business cards you've collected.

Create one pile for potential clients, one for potential team members, one for potential referral partners, and one for potential collaborative partners. (If you don't know which pile to put a person in, use the body compass exercise you've been practicing throughout this book.)

- **Enter all the cards into your database** with notes about each contact. *Note: Do not add people to your email distribution list without prior approval! This is considered "spammy," and tends to make people angry.*

- **Send a "nice to meet you" email or snail mail card** to each person you met. Mention one thing that stood out about your conversation. Check in with your Highest Self before writing each note to see if there is something in particular that person needs to hear from you.

- **Within 48 hours, call to schedule a follow-up** coffee with those you are really drawn to. Trust your gut, here. After meeting with someone you feel might belong in your tribe, invite them to schedule a complimentary sales call.

- **In your database, track your follow up with each person** and the outcome. Use that tracking to refine the events you'll attend in the future.

Love-Based Feminine Marketing:

Chapter 18
MARKETING STRATEGY 3: CONTENT MARKETING

I sit in front of my computer, my finger hovering over the send button.

Should I do it?

I weigh the risks.

Others have urged me to give it a try. It will "make your life so much easier," they say. "We could communicate so much faster!"

On the other hand, my business books are on this computer. I track every hour and every penny spent on a job. I also have our bank account records saved. If anyone gets ahold of those things, we (no, I) will be in so much trouble.

And that would be an emotional beating. Maybe even inspire physical retribution, as well.

I go back and forth, knots growing in my belly.

Finally, I take the chance. I push send.

It was the early 1990s, and I had just sent my first email.

Fast forward to 2011 and I hadn't progressed far! I used Facebook to check up on my world-roaming young-adult children, just to make sure they were still alive. I had a very basic LinkedIn profile, because someone else set it up as a favor to me. I sent occasional emails about my business to people I knew. And that was it.

I had built a small coaching practice through networking. I was happy! It was comfortable. I brought in a little bit of money that allowed me to pay my bills and not have to work a full-time j-o-b. I liked money, but I had been told that the way to grow my business was to find people's fear and twist it! Make them believe I was the only answer to their biggest problems and they can't survive without me.

I refused. Instinctively, I knew it would wreck me. It wasn't who I was, or who I wanted to become.

So, I stayed small and local. I sometimes fantasized about a six-figure income, but the cost seemed too high.

Then, the housing crisis hit, and it hit hard.

A few years earlier, my new husband (the one my Highest Self had promised I'd meet all those years ago ... the soul who would come along to support and love me so beautifully in this work) had started his own land-use business.

He worked with owners and developers to secure permissions needed to build development projects on the Central Coast.

Attorneys, architects, and engineers often called to ask for his assistance. His practice was small, but profitable.

Until it wasn't.

Thanks to the housing crisis, larger developers finished what they were working on (or not) and left town. Most left plans on the table. Investment money dried up. No one was building or planning to build.

My husband still had a few projects—private clients and businesses in need of support. But new work stopped coming in. We borrowed against his retirement to keep going.

The final blow came when his last client decided to bankrupt the California arm of their business and default on all payments. They still had their East Coast properties, which were much more profitable. Still, they let us know they would not be paying their bill … ever. We were out tens of thousands of dollars.

He started looking for a job.

Suddenly, money was really tight. I knew if nothing changed, nothing *would* change. So, I unfroze my emergency credit card and hired a coach to learn to market in a way that felt true and authentic to who I am … the love-based way!

And that's when I was introduced to the gorilla that IS content marketing. It was fun, but scary. In the beginning, I had no idea what I was doing. Slowly, though, over time, I found my way.

As times have changed, I've adapted, and my business has grown. (For example, while I once used Google+ and Pinterest as my main social media outlets, I now focus on Facebook and Instagram. Now, if your first response to hearing anything about social media is something like, "I don't do Facebook," that's ok. Neither did I. But it is one of the primary engines of my marketing program today, and a big part of what makes my business successful, so try and keep an open mind.)

Content marketing includes your:

- Blog

- Newsletter

- Youtube or other video-hosting site

- Podcast or radio show

- Other online marketing outlets

Reading all of that can be pretty overwhelming, I know.

So, take three deep belly breaths. Settle your Saboteurs.

We start simply, by allowing your Highest Self and the Energy of Your Business to guide you.

Again, this is a place where your Divine Masculine gets to serve your Divine Feminine. So, your feminine, creative self will create the content, and your masculine self will create a container for that content.

Step 1: Create the Container.

- Set up a page on your website to post your blog (most sites already have a designated page). Have your website designer or a techy friend help if you don't have the expertise to do it yourself. (This is a good place to practice the skill of receiving, which will help you in receiving more money as you grow your business.)

- Subscribe to a content-management system that will store the names and emails of your followers. (This is what you'll use to schedule your newsletters to be sent. SurveyMonkey is a good first system.)

- Research social media sites. Yep, you finally get to do some physical world research. Because social media is such a big part of the physical world today, it will be easy for you to do a quick online search and come up with quite a few interesting sites. (Don't worry … you won't be posting to all of them.)

A few of the top platforms include:

Facebook: Currently, it's the "biggest" social media platform with 2.41 billion users as of the second quarter of 2019. Just about everybody and their grandma are on Facebook! Unless your target market is the youth generation, you will probably be able to reach them through Facebook.

Think about Facebook as a great big worldwide cocktail/networking event. It's a place where you can let down your hair and be real (keeping in mind that it *is* still a public platform).

Somewhere on Facebook, your perfect client is scrolling her feed looking for something interesting. That could be you!

LinkedIn: The professional suit-and-tie platform. It's especially useful for business-to-business service providers. LinkedIn is used to build a network of people who will recommend your services to others. (It could also be where you find someone with the perfect skill set to assist you as you grow your business.)

YouTube: *The* place to post your videos. Videos rank high in Google searches, so you show up near the top of the list when someone searches for the services you provide. Videos allow you teach, sell, build an audience, and connect with your peeps.

Did you know that website visitors who watch a video are 64% more likely to make a purchase than those who don't? Videos let your potential clients see the real you. You can create a heart connection through video that is much more difficult to do with just words. If one picture is worth 1000 words, how much more valuable is a one-minute video?

Pinterest: For businesses that have a very visual aspect (photographers, designers, fashion, food, and travel businesses). Pinterest's audience is primarily women, so if women are your demographic, this could be "it" for you.

Plus, people will buy from Pinterest, so it's a good place to showcase products.

Instagram: With over a billion active monthly users, this is a *huge* platform! It relies on visual storytelling, which connects instantly to the heart. People buy based on their emotions. Tell a good story on Instagram and your chances of finding new clients increase dramatically.

Step 2: Using Your Body Compass, Choose FACEBOOK and One Other Social Media Platform to Focus On.

* Yes, I am telling you to use Facebook ... because it's the mother f*3king elephant of social media! It's highly probable that somewhere on Facebook, there are people who need what you offer.

**The exception to the Facebook rule is when your Highest Self and your Inner Mastermind Council repeatedly tell you it's in your highest and best good to ignore Facebook. If this is the case, you'll need to be diligent in using other platforms.

Step 3: Prepare Your Social Media Accounts.

- Set up your accounts on each platform.

- Block out time on your calendar for social media activities using the "Chunk It Up" action tool:

- Set aside 15 minutes per day to work on social media posts (wondering what to post? Keep reading), etc. (Everyone can find 15 minutes and, keeping the timeframe short will also help keep you from becoming overwhelmed, or swallowed up by the Social Media Time-Suck Black Hole!)

- Set a timer so you won't be tempted to spend more than 15 minutes.

- Stop after 15 minutes, even if you are on a roll. This creates a success habit, training your brain to work in short chunks toward a long-term goal.

When you plan to work for 15 minutes, but then work beyond that self-imposed limit, your subconscious brain learns to distrust. It considers your plans lies. And then, the next day, when you get ready to do your 15 minutes, your subconscious brain will say, "*Ha ha! I know how you are, self. I don't have two hours to spend on this. I'll put it off for now.*"

And alas, you will find yourself putting the work off for days and days, rather than enjoying continuous daily progress.

Step 4: Create Your Content.

Content refers to a combination of information and inspiration that you use to connect with your audience.

Set a regular time and place to get into the practice of creating content. In the beginning, it may be uncomfortable for you, especially if those Saboteurs come out to play. I promise, it will get easier the more you do it!

Tips for Creating Content:

Tip 1: Begin by using the meditation in Chapter 11 to connect with your Tribal Representative. Ask what your tribe most needs to hear from you in that moment. What would be of greatest use?

Tip 2: Notice what's up in your life. How does it tie into what your tribe needs to hear? Is there something happening that relates to what your Tribal Rep told you?

Tip 3: Write a first (crappy) draft of whatever it is you want to share with others. Seriously! Don't expect it to be good the first time. It won't be. Just get the thoughts on paper.

Tip 4: Go back and edit. Have someone else edit. Do a final edit yourself.

Tips for Writing Social Media and Blog Posts:

Think of your blog posts as love letters to your tribe. This is your chance to court your next client! It's also the first act of service you provide AND a great way to spread your message.

Begin by writing twice a month until you are comfortable expanding into a weekly blog, which will keep you "top of mind" to your followers.

Tip 1. You MUST get personal. People want to feel a connection to YOU. They want to get to know YOU. There is a ton of information in the world, so you can't deliver a teaching until you have their attention. This is where STORY comes into play.

Tip 2. Start with YOUR story. Write as if you were telling your best friend. "Dear Sue, this happened to me!" Follow Joseph Campbell's archetypical hero's journey, which has several stages. Think about the journey of Luke in the Star Wars trilogy or Frodo Baggins in the Hobbit. Both follow the complex journey, from reluctant traveler of many quests to the hero returned.

A blog post is generally between 300 and 700 words. This isn't really enough space for the whole journey, so include a **reluctant hero** (you or a client), **a challenge**, how you (or the client) **overcame it**, and how great your (his or her) life is as a **result**. Write from your heart and sprinkle in some of your **marketing words**.

Tip 3. Provide one teaching nugget. What can the reader learn from reading the story? What did the energetic rep ask for?

Tip 4. Add your CTA (Call To Action). *"I invite you to consider scheduling a complimentary call with me to see if I'm the person to help you get more of what you want ... like the person in the story above."*

General Copywriting Tips:

- Write short paragraphs consisting of one to three sentences each. Short sentences: no more than 17 words in any sentence.

- Write at a seventh-grade level.

- Write to one person, not to the masses.

- Use CAPITALIZATION, **bolding**, *italicizing*, larger and colored font to make important ideas and thoughts stand out.

- Use wide margins on the right side to create shorter, easier to read lines.

- Add photos. This enhances the message and engages at a deeper level. Photos of you are especially important to help your audience with the "know, like, trust factor." Use a combination of professional photos and selfies.

- Be consistent. RELAX and have fun! Your style and writing will evolve over time as your audience gets to know you.

Step 5: Leverage.

This step is about getting your content out there as much as possible.

- Post what you create to your website blog.

- Email it to your list as either a solo email (with no other content attached) or as a part of your newsletter.

- Use a subject line that will capture interest. "Dog bites man" is not a story, but "Man bites dog" is! Create a "Man Bites Dog" type of subject line.

- Post it to your social media accounts. **Note: for Facebook, do not put links in the body of the post. They must be put in the comments section.**

- Tag friends and followers who are most likely to enjoy and comment on your post. The more comments you receive, the more widely Facebook distributes the post.

- Bonus tip: Create a blog circle of trusted colleagues who agree to comment on each other's posts thoughtfully once a week or more. Tag them!

- Use quotes and tidbits from your post to create additional social media memes to be used throughout the week.

Once you've mastered the habit of content creation, leverage becomes easy. You can even hand over posting, creating quotes, and asking for comments to a team member, so that all *you* are doing is creating the original post.

Talk about leveraging your time!

Love-Based Feminine Marketing:

Chapter 19
MARKETING STRATEGY 4: ESTABLISHING EXPERTISE FROM THE STAGE

"It's time," I say, *"for you to stand in front of the room and share your wisdom."*

My client agrees. Yet, there is a catch in her voice. Her energy drops. I feel my own throat tighten.

She goes into a coughing fit.

When she speaks again, her voice is rough and shallow.

"What is happening in your throat?" I ask.

This is a seasoned client. She has done a lot of inner work. She is strong, smart, and oh so wise. She knows where to look.

"There is a dragon," she tells me, *"wrapped around my throat. He doesn't want me to speak. He doesn't want me to take the stage."*

"Dragon," I ask, *"How long have you been with her?"*

"A long, long time," the woman says, allowing dragon to speak through her. I hear his voice in my head, deep and rumbly. His breath is hot. I know he has fire in him.

"What is your purpose?" I ask.

"To protect her from the wrath of her grandmother," he whispers. Her voice cracks just a little; his reverberates in the spirit plane.

"I thought I had dealt with this already," she says, tears starting to fall. *"I thought I was done with that woman."*

Then, she tells me the story. She was five; it was the holiday season, and she had a poem to recite on stage all on her own. When the time came for her to speak, she stood tall and began her recitation. She got to the last two lines and froze. She couldn't remember them and looked to her teacher in the wings. Her teacher gave her the first two words, and off she went to complete the poem. The applause was thunderous—she even received a standing ovation!

Her parents came backstage to give her hugs and high praise. However, her grandmother just stood back and scowled. She asked what was the wrong, and her grandmother answered, *"You should never speak in front of people again. You just aren't very good at it!!"*

As a result, that five-year-old created a dragon that would stop her if she ever tried. The dragon, then, would save her from future embarrassment and shame and, most importantly, from the anger of her grandmother.

And for 50 years, dragon had done his job, painfully letting go only when she insisted on speaking at meetings, trainings, and other such events.

There she was, full well knowing that the only way for her business to grow to the next level was to become the expert in front of the room. Whereas networking connected her one-on-one to prospects, speaking would position her in front of many. Plus, being a speaker automatically infers expertise.

In other words, *she needed her voice back full time,* starting right then.

So, we began looking for any cords or hooks that her grandmother, long dead, had embedded in her. She removed the cords and filled the holes with love and healing. She told her grandmother that she was no longer welcome in her head, and her grandmother's message of silence was sent back.

Then, she spoke with the dragon. He agreed to be her advocate, lending her his fire when she spoke, so her message would carry farther.

Today, she is the host of one of the most successful radio programs on Voice America! She speaks regularly at events around the world and even facilitates her own live events several times a year.

She is brilliant, funny, and highly engaging. AND, she loves it!

Her story is not unusual. The details are hers, but the belief that "good girls should be seen and not heard" still permeates our society. And again, the idea that women should grow up and be obedient wives still lives in our DNA.

The suffragettes were considered "less than feminine" because they dared to voice an opinion. It was believed that there was something wrong with them physically, too. (After all, no normal woman would want to vote!)

Today, when women speak, their voices are criticized, demeaned, and trolled horribly. So, it is natural for Fear to pop up.

Yet we must, must, speak. We must tell our stories, share our purpose. In the process, our businesses will grow. We will create our movements. We will change the world for our daughters and granddaughters.

We must get our message out there!

Let's start by thinking about how to get you onstage.

Speaking opportunities include:

- Speaking in person at other people's events (i.e. networking events, conferences, rotary clubs, etc.—anywhere your tribe regularly gathers).

- Speaking in person at your own events (monthly meetings, workshops, multiday live events).

- Speaking virtually on other people's online platforms (radio shows, podcasts, telesummits, etc.).

- Speaking virtually on your own online platforms (radio shows, podcasts, telesummits, Facebook Lives, etc.).

Since you're going to want to take every opportunity you can to practice your signature talk, this is where you reach out to people you know and ask for help. If the person doesn't think your talk is a fit for her group, be sure to ask if she knows anyone who might be interested in what you have to share (you'll do this after completing the steps below). You can also research groups on meetup.com. Ask in your Facebook groups if anyone is seeking speakers. Rotary groups are a good place to get practice, too. They meet weekly and are always in need of speakers. And don't forget the power of a simple google search!

Once you have ideas as to where you'll speak, you have to know what you're going to say.

Here's the deal:

You'll want to create three to four signature talks that will identify you as the expert in your field. This will allow you to focus on your niche, and not waste time recreating a talk every time you are booked.

Start with one. Get good at it. Share it (and thereby, your expertise) widely. Get known as "the (insert your niche) woman."

From there, you can create your second (and then, after you repeat the process, your third) talk, still seeped in your niche. Remember, your goal is to speak to the heart of those in your audience who are meant to be served by you. Don't be seduced into speaking outside your niche just because someone wants you to. It may feel good, but it will ultimately distract you and keep your business from growing ... and the money from flowing.

Right now, you're probably thinking something like, "Well this sounds great, Julie. Now, how in the world do I create my signature talk?"

You complete this exercise to get started, of course. (This is a fun one to complete with a friend or past client who knows your work, too.)

Exercise: Creating Your Signature Talk

Grab your journal and pen.

Step 1: Brainstorm a list of topics. List everything you could possibly talk about. Add your silly ideas, and the ones you would never dare talk about out loud. Even if you can't imagine sharing them, write them down anyway. They act as lubricant for your most amazing ideas to come out of hiding!

Step 2: Have a conversation with your Tribal Representative to discuss which topics would be most appealing. Which would draw her to book an appointment to explore working with you?

Step 3: Have a conversation with the Energy of Your Business. First, narrow the list of topics you've created down to the three that most light up your business. Take each idea into your heart. Which one feels the most alive? Which are you most confident about? Which idea makes your business dance with joy? Run them past the Energy of Your Business and see what response you get.

Step 4: Chunk it up. Choose the first topic you're going to work on and start getting all of your talking points on paper (use bullet points for your brainstorming). You want three to five main talking points for your topic.

Then, name the "why." For each bullet point, describe a physical-world benefit for learning the point you're sharing. Make it as specific as possible. Yes, "so you can be empowered" is a nice combination of words; however, "so you can make more money with more ease" is a more concrete benefit.

Step 5: Write a first draft.

Here is a structure you can use to draft your talk:

Begin your talk with an interesting fact or story. Don't do the "thank you for being here" thing. Jump right into content that is interesting. (Side note: "Give yourself a pat on the back for being here" is not interesting, but it *is* annoying!)

Tell a little bit about your personal story. Why are you the perfect person to talk to your audience about your topic?

Share your bullet points, expanding on each. Make sure you give a few action steps your audience members can take as soon as they leave to implement the bullet points you teach them.

Provide *great* information. You want to highlight the best of you, so your listeners are drawn to you. Position your talk as "Here are the first steps; you get more when you work with me."

End with a call to action. A simple example: "I hope this information has been helpful. For some of you, this is all you need. For those of you who want more, I have room in my calendar for five complimentary exploratory calls, so we can explore how I might best serve you. I'll be at the back of the room and will schedule one of these calls with each of the first five who meet me there."

Step 6: Create a speaker one-sheet (remember, you can go here to download a copy of this sheet: HTTPS://JULIEFOUCHT.COM/FMRESOURCES/). A speaker one-sheet is a professional PDF or printed document that allows speaker bookers to scan your information and see if you are someone they would like to book. Your speaker one-sheet includes the name of your talk, your bullet points, a brief bio that speaks to your expertise in the area of your topic, and testimonials. You should also include your professional headshot.

Here's a template you can print out or use to create your own one-sheet:

Your Name Speaker and Author Your expertise	Your headshot
Your contact info	
Your Talk Title	Your bio
*45 minute *90 minute * Keynote * Workshop or Interview format available* A short paragraph about your talk Participants will discover: ✔ Bullet point take away ✔ Bullet point take away ✔ Bullet point take away ✔ Bullet point take away ✔ Bullet point take away	
➜ Testimonial	

Bonus tip: Once you have the content for your one-sheet written, hire a graphic designer to make it look professional. If you don't have a graphic person on your team, check out fiverr.com. You can preview the work of several designers and the prices are inexpensive enough to allow you to hire two or three people to create a one-sheet for you, so you can choose and use your favorite. (And if you find someone whose work you love, save his or her name, so you can find him/her again next time you need graphic work.)

Step 7: Create a reach-out letter template (go here to download this template: JULIEFOUCHT.COM/FMRESOURCES).

Create a template reach-out letter, so you aren't starting from scratch each time you're interested in a speaking opportunity. Then, you can simply customize it to the person or group.

This is another place you can utilize a team as your business grows. You can assign one person to find speaking gigs for you, then, all you do is show up and share your wisdom.

Here is a sample reach out letter you can customize to your own:

Hi Name,

My name is (your name). I'm reaching out to see if I might be a fit for speaking at your upcoming event, (name of their event).

I have a program called (the name of your signature talk in bold so it stands out) that may be a good fit for your group.

My message is a unique approach on (one to two sentences about your topic—you can use the talk description you created for your speaker one-sheet).

In all of my keynotes, I use personal stories and humor to clarify key points while giving the audience powerful strategies that can be implemented right away to create immediate results.

My mission is (name your mission and explain how it will benefit their group).

Please feel free to contact me via email at (your email.com or on my cell phone at XXX-XXX-XXXX).

Thank you for your time. I look forward to the possible opportunity to serve your group.

Warmest Regards,

SIGNATURE

NAME

Step 8: Decide how far you're willing to travel. Create a spreadsheet of organizations or groups you might speak to within that radius. Note how many members they have, how often they meet, and the location.

Step 9: Create a schedule for reaching out and following up. Send a reach-out letter and your speaker one-sheet to every connection you make. Note any response you receive. If you don't receive a response, follow up in a week.

Step 10: Memorize the beginning and end of your talk. Memorize the bullet points, too, and practice talking about each one. Avoid scripting and memorizing the whole thing, though, as doing so will likely come off as stilted and insincere.

Finally, here are some "bonus tips" for taking the stage:

Tip 1: Who you BE on stage is just as important as what you say.

Tip 2: You will naturally feel some nervousness, no matter how practiced you are. Find a quiet place, like the bathroom, where you can take a few moments. Take three deep belly breaths. Invite your Highest Self to join you. Feel her with you. Let the little girl inside of you go play.

As you feel your Highest Self, smile and get in "superwoman pose": feet shoulder width apart, hands raised in victory. Puff out your chest, pull back your shoulders. Feel your power.

Tip 3: As you take the stage, pause. Plant your feet shoulder width apart. Feel roots growing from your feet into Mama Earth. Feel her energy flowing up through your feet, grounding you, nourishing you. During your talk, move around the stage with purpose, spending most of the time with your feet planted (wandering shows nervousness).

Take a few more seconds to scan the audience. Connect with as many eyes as possible. As you connect, send a golden thread from your heart to theirs. If there are audience members still chatting or staring at their phone, simply wait, your eyes on their faces, until you have everyone's attention.

Tip 4: Begin with your prepared opening. If you are really nervous, be transparent. Let them know you are nervous. Then, open your talk anyway.

Love-Based Feminine Marketing:

Chapter 20
MAKING FRIENDS WITH MONEY

Being your own boss is the greatest personal development course in the world. It requires you to step out of your comfort zone, release old patterns and beliefs, let go of emotional baggage, and BE the highest version of yourself.

It's been one of the best experiences of my life!

But let's be real, here: if you aren't making money, you aren't staying in business for long.

The good news is that the spiritual universe is set up so that you *can* win big at the money game … *if* you are willing to follow your own path.

The final chapter in our journey here is all about your relationship with the Energy of Money. (Incidentally, as I write this, I'm on an airplane on my way to Cabo San Lucas to lead a retreat about money!)

I'm *passionate* about women having access to *lots* of money.

Because when they do, *they have choice.*

They can choose to stay in a marriage or leave.

They can choose to give to causes they believe in.

They get a seat at the table of decision makers.

The truth is, Money loves you.

Money wants to spend time with you.

Money wants to be used by you to live a vibrant, juicy life.

Money wants to partner with you to bring more joy and healing to the planet.

Money needs you to be the channel through which it can flow into the world.

As I've mentioned, for generations now, women have been taught to be "nice" and "marriageable." That their best chance at a good life comes from their ability to attract a successful husband.

Again, WE CARRY THAT MESSAGE IN OUR DNA!

We have never been taught to be wealthy.

We have never been taught to be abundant.

We have been taught that money is limited, and resources are to be fought over.

The truth is, money is an energy of appreciation. In our society, we track that as dollar bills and coins. It is used as an exchange of equal value. And, that energy, like love, is unlimited.

Just as you can speak with the Energy of Your Business, you can speak with the Energy of Money—AND you should, because the Energy of Money needs you as a channel for doing its work in the world.

Money is meant to elevate humanity.

Yet, it can't do anything without the right hands, the right stewards, to pass through.

And as it passes through, it gives generously.

Yeah babe …

Money wants to bless you, be used by you, be in LOVE with you!

Money wants a kind and uplifting relationship.

It's this simple: a relationship grows through communication.

Yet, the only relationship most people have with Money is negative. They worry about not having enough; they stress over paying the bills; they complain about the high price of everything.

And Money is left feeling small, powerless, and unappreciated.

The problem is, Money wants to go where it is appreciated, acknowledged, respected.

Think about it ... you wouldn't treat a friend or lover the way you treat Money, would you?

One of the keys to The Art of Feminine Marketing is to create a strong, sustainable, connected relationship with the Energy of Money.

And one of the primary techniques I've used to build a great relationship with Money is to have regular conversations with the Energy of Money.

Doing so has enabled me to create a business through which I work very closely with high-end clients, travel all over the country with them, vacation a lot, and purchase my dream home.

I've courted Money, gotten to know it well, been surprised by some of the things it taught me, and been really, really blessed by the opportunities it's brought.

Exercise: 7 Days of Courting Money

This is a seven-day process that you can repeat as many times as you want. Each day takes you deeper into the process, and each time your repeat the seven-day cycle, your connection to money, and your ability to receive, deepens.

Put your journal and pen in your designated space or, create a folder on your computer to hold your writing for each day.

Invite a friend to join you in the process and be your accountability partner! Having someone you trust read or listen to what you've written will help you to get more from the experience.

Set your mind to relax and, have fun!

Step 1: Prepare.

Set up a designated space to go through the process each and every day at a designated time (otherwise, you risk putting it off and perhaps never getting to it). This can be anywhere: at your desk, your altar space, your comfy tea corner, even your favorite coffee shop. Add sacred items to your space to help spark your connection to Source.

Step 2: Invite the Energy of Money to join you.

Simply state, "Money, I invite you to join me."

 Step 3: Review the daily affirmation and question (see below).

Step 4: When you're ready, write it.

Write the affirmation in your money journal and read it aloud. Focus your attention on the affirmation. What comes up for you? What feelings, thoughts, and/or old beliefs pop into your head? Simply notice them without judgement.

Write the question in your journal and allow the Energy of Money to respond.

Keep writing. Write whatever answer pops into your head without editing. If additional questions come up, or you want to explore more with Money, continue the conversation. Each question is a new opportunity for you to get to know Money better.

Courting Money Daily Prompts (print them out here JULIEFOUCHT.COM/FMRESOURCES):

Day 1 Affirmation: Source is my source. I am one with and connected to Source energy. I vibrate in harmony with this knowledge creating the energy needed to make all of my desires manifest in the physical reality. This is the source of all of my prosperity.

Day 1 Question: Money, can you tell me about prosperity?

Day 2 Affirmation: Money is a physical expression of appreciation sourced from Source. When I allow money to flow through me in an attitude of thankfulness, it is magnified, and I attract more of what my soul desires.

Day 2 Question: Money, can you tell me how you move through me for the highest good?

Day 3 Affirmation: Money needs me, loves me, wants to be with me, and wants to be used by me to create more love in the world. Money is my partner in fulfilling my mission on the planet.

Day 3 Question: Money, how we can be better partners and friends?

Day 4 Affirmation: Source provides for all my needs, allowing money to flow to me through many different doors and channels. I am happy and grateful for each expression of Source's love for me, for the abundance I experience today, and the abundance that is coming.

Day 4 Question: Money, what do I need to know in order to open even more doors of abundance?

Day 5 Affirmation: Money wants me to live a vibrant, juicy, fulfilling life. It is through me that money expresses its true purpose: to elevate and better all of humanity. When I am happy and vibrant, it raises my vibration. This, in turn, raises the vibration of those around me, creating ripples of healing throughout the world. I choose to spend money in ways that raise my vibration.

Day 5 Question: Money, what do I need to release in order to have more of you?

Day 6 Affirmation: I gladly and gratefully receive appreciation for the work I do in the form of money. When I partner with money this way, the value of my work is magnified, blessing those I serve exponentially.

Day 6 Question: Money, can you tell me about my value in the world?

Day 7 Affirmation: I am grateful for the money that flows through me. I am constantly growing in my understanding and expanding my ability to receive more abundance. I share joyfully, with the deep knowledge that my success elevates others, as their success elevates me.

Day 7 Question: Money, can you tell me how you would like to be used by me?

Chapter 21
HOW GOOD CAN YOU STAND IT?

The night air is soft and warm. The desert is so quiet, I can almost hear the sea on the horizon.

We've let the darkness catch us and no one has felt the need to turn on the lights.

I can barely make out the shape of my co-facilitator at the edge of the infinity pool. The one client who has stayed a day after the retreat is lying on a lounge chair, still processing her transformation.

I lie back as well and count the stars. Source speaks to me of possibilities, of the work we have just completed, of the difference the women will now make in the world. My heart is filled with gratitude.

I feel my Highest Self urging me to rise, to turn on the music. The Energy of Money wants to dance.

I scroll through my phone and choose a song. Anything Is Possible by Jen Hannah.

We dance.

I move my hips, my arms, my feet. I feel the words twining around my soul, "Anything is possible." I begin to cry.

I flash back to my coach's training. I was, at that time, just coming out of the pain of my divorce. I was beginning to feel strong again. Powerful. I was learning my purpose ... that I am the creator of my life. I knew I wanted to create something magical.

Our instructors led us on an inner journey to meet our future selves. I had been meditating for years, so I dropped easily into that journey. First, out into space, then following a beam of light back down to earth 20 years into the future.

I met my future self—the woman I am becoming. She stood in the doorway of a beautiful home, a wall of glass doors pushed all the way open, so the ocean breeze billowed in her clothing. All around her were amazing, world-changing truthtellers—women who had come to Mexico to study with her, to experience her magic healing.

She looked out at the infinity pool and desert beyond.

"This," she whispers, "this is your future."

The moment becomes the moment as I dance and cry. The house I envisioned is the house I now dance in. The pool in the vision is the pool in which my co-facilitator pirouettes. It has only been 14 years, not 20, but I have arrived at the future I dreamed of!

All the hair on my body stands on end. My breath catches. I sigh in delight.

Holy F*(k!, I think. I did it.

All of the tools that I've shared in this book have brought me to this place.

My vision continues to expand and pull me forward with it and my dreams are now bigger and bolder. I don't know how it will all happen, but I trust that the way will reveal itself if I continue to follow my own path.

And it will for you too, sister.

As W.H. Murray, member of the second Himalayan Expedition said, "Until one is committed, there is hesitancy, the chance to draw back, always ineffective. Concerning all acts of initiative (and creation), there is one elementary truth the ignorance of which kills countless ideas and splendid plans: that the moment one definitely commits oneself, then Providence moves too. All sorts of things occur to help one that would never otherwise have occurred. A whole stream of events issues from the decision, raising in one's favor all manner of unforeseen incidents and meeting and material assistance which no man could have dreamed would have come his way."

Dear sister, begin. Take the first right step. Use the tools that you've learned in this book, or don't. But DO begin.

Love-Based Feminine Marketing:

RESOURCES

The following resources can be found at https://juliefoucht.com/fmresources/:

Connect with Your Highest Self Guided Meditation

Connect with Your Business Guided Meditation

Discovering Your Wounds Timeline

Connect with the Energy of Your Perfect Tribe Guided Meditation

Moving Past Resistance

Connect with Your Body Singer Guided Meditation

Assembling Your Inner Mastermind Counsel Guided Meditation

Make a Spiritual Connection Guided Meditation

Send a Spiritual Invite Guided Meditation

Speaker One-Sheet Template

Reach-out Letter Template

Love-Based Feminine Marketing:

Other books in the Love-Based Business Series

Love-Based Copywriting Method: The Philosophy Behind Writing Copy That Attracts, Inspires and Invites
(Volume 1 in the Love-Based Business Series)
By Michele PW

This book is a great place to learn more about the philosophy behind love-based copy and love-based selling. While it does include many exercises, it's more focused on the love-based philosophy and building a solid love-based foundation. If you're looking for a "how-to write love-based copy" book, definitely check out the next one in the series.

lovebasedpublishing.com/book/love-based-copywriting-method

Love-Based Copywriting System: A Step-by-Step Process to Master Writing Copy That Attracts, Inspires and Invites
(Volume 2 in the Love-Based Business Series)
By Michele PW

This is a copywriting course in book format. This "how to" book walks you through exactly how to write love-based copy. It includes exercises, copy templates and more. If you're planning on doing any sort of writing for your business—for instance, writing emails or website copy—this book is a must-have.

lovebasedpublishing.com/book/love-based-copywriting-system

Love-Based Online Marketing: Campaigns to Grow a Business You Love AND That Loves You Back
(Volume 3 in the Love-Based Business Series)
By Michele PW

All successful, profitable businesses need a marketing plan, and this book walks you through how to create one that is perfect for you. You'll also learn the basics of selingl products and services online without feeling sales-y, and what might be standing in your way of successfully marketing your business.

lovebasedpublishing.com/book/love-based-online-marketing

Love-Based Money and Mindset: Make the Money You Desire Without Selling Your Soul
(Volume 4 in the Love-Based Business Series)
By Michele PW

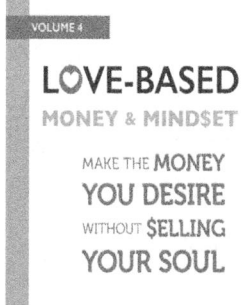

Are you ready to step into a life of peaceful prosperity? "Love-Based Money and Mindset" is designed to help you heal your relationship with money so you not only feel peaceful about it, but you're also able to attract all the abundance you want.

While this book is designed to help everyone who struggles with money issues, it's particularly helpful for those who have (or want to have) a business. The bottom line: the more you can cultivate a love-based mindset, the more easily and effortlessly you'll attract money into your life.

lovebasedpublishing.com/book/love-based-money-mindset

Love-Based Goals: Your Guide to Living Your Purpose & Passion
(Volume 5 in the Love-Based Business Series)
By Michele PW

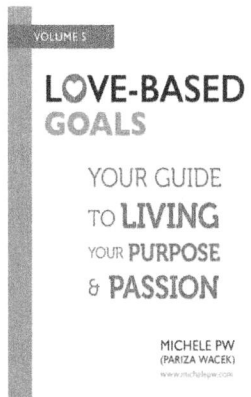

If you're ready to step into the life of your dreams and do it with ease and grace, this book can help. You'll get the tools you need to discover your love-based goals, get clear on what's stopping you and create an individualized plan to help you finally start living your dream life.

lovebasedpublishing.com/book/love-based-goals

Love-Based Business Models: A Simple System For Bulding A Business You Love
(Volume 6 in the Love-Based Business Series)
By Shawn Driscoll

In this book, Business Coach Shawn Driscoll teaches you the philosophy and the foundational principles behind creating business models that fit with and support your life, priorities, interests, demands, strengths, and weaknesses. Whether you're a seasoned entrepreneur or you're just starting out, you'll discover practical tips and strategies for identifying and building a business around your unique strengths and your mission, using a model that maximizes your impact and supports everything that's important to you.

lovebasedpublishing.com/love-based-series/business-models

Love-Based Mission: How to Create a Business That Serves Your Soul
(Volume 7 in the Love-Based Business Series)
By Therese Skelly

You've probably heard it before: Running a business is the very best way to fast-track your personal growth. According to Therese Skelly, author of Love-Based Mission: How to Create a Business That Serves Your Soul, the entrepreneurial journey is also a spiritual path. And becoming a love-based business owner will change your life! There is something specific that you and you alone are here to do for the world. It's your soul's purpose for your life. Now, it's up to you to become the steward of that work! In the pages of this book, you'll uncover what holds you back and discover who you must be to birth your mission-driven business. You'll learn how to reach the personal and spiritual transformation you seek, along the way. The bottom line? Not only is it possible to learn to love your business, but even more importantly, you can learn to love yourself in an even deeper way.

lovebasedpublishing.com/love-based-series/love-based-mission

Love-Based Feminine Marketing:

How to Start a Business You Love AND That Loves You Back: Get Clear on Your Purpose & Passion - Build a Successful, Profitable Business
Part of the Love-Based Business Series
By Michele PW

This book includes exercises and questions to ask yourself to make sure the heart of your business reflects what you really want it to. It's about answering the deeper questions around your business, like why you want it in the first place—because the clearer you are in your answers to those questions, the more satisfied you'll most likely be with what you eventually build.

Michele wrote this book for you if you don't have a business yet, but you want to get started, and you're intrigued by the idea of having a business you love and that loves you back.

Get it for FREE, here:

lovebasedpublishing.com/book/how-to-start-a-biz-you-love

About the Author
ABOUT JULIE FOUCHT

When Julie Foucht decided she needed to take her coaching business seriously, she hired a high-end coach and learned to "market like a man." She doubled, then tripled, her income in less than a year, but felt drained, uninspired, and restless.

Urged by Spirit, she embraced her essential 'Womaness' and birthed a new way, The Art of Feminine Marketing.

Today, Julie teaches female coaches, teachers, and healers who are frustrated with traditional marketing how to build six-figure businesses that honor their feminine essence.

Julie's clients report having clearer vision of their divine purpose, greater passion for their work, the skills to attract the perfect clients, and profits in exchange for their gifts.

Julie received her coach certification in 2006 from The Coaches Training Institute. She has served on the boards of numerous non-profits and was named Woman of the Year by the Professional Women's Network of the Monterey Peninsula in 2013.

She is married to the love of her life, has four children, two stepchildren, two furry babies, and seven (spoiled) grandchildren.

The Art of Growing a 6-Figure Business Without Hustle, Grind, or Force

Made in the USA
Columbia, SC
12 August 2020